NOAH
Grants
HOPE

NOAH *Grants* HOPE

231 Days of a Mother's Transformation Post-Lifequake

Dr. Tiffany Ryan

SYNERGY
PUBLISHING GROUP

BELMONT, NORTH CAROLINA

Noah Grants Hope: 231 Days of a Mother's
Transformation Post-Lifequake
Dr. Tiffany Ryan

Published by Synergy Publishing Group, Belmont, NC
Layout and design by Melisa Graham

Softcover, July 2025, ISBN 978-1-960892-49-2
E-book, July 2025, ISBN 978-1-960892-50-8

To my beautiful children—Noah, Grant, and Hope. You have been, are, and always will be the greatest joys and teachers of my life. I am eternally grateful you chose me to be your mom on this spin around the sun. I love you more than you'll ever know.

Contents

Introduction:
Months 1 & 2
Post-Lifequake

I am a mom. A teacher. A researcher. A wellness enthusiast. And now, I suppose a writer *and* mother living without her firstborn son being physically present.

In the first two months after my son, Noah, transitioned out of his body in July of 2024, and leading up to publicly acknowledging that my son had died by suicide, I spent my days lying in a hammock in the backyard, staring, pondering, and reading. I would consistently have flashes of insight or existential and philosophical questions pop into my head. Eventually, I decided to start writing them down because my brain was on overload trying to comprehend and keep track of all of them. Entire days were consumed with trying to make sense of what had just happened. Trying to make sense of how I was supposed to continue living without my son. My therapist even encouraged me to get a huge whiteboard where I could write it all down and visually make the connections my brain was trying to understand.

I believe these insights and existential inquiries were spurred by my need and quest to figure out how to survive. I was fearful most of the day, for months. Fearful of my life. Of being awake. Of sleeping. Of my existence. Of what might have happened to Noah before, during, and after his death. Of what might happen in the future to me and my still Earth-side kids. Of my kids being permanently damaged by this trauma. Of being alone. Of seeing and talking to people who made it more real. Of not seeing a way through this life and needing to die myself. Fearful of fully connecting with Noah's spirit. Fearful of not fully connecting with his spirit. Fearful of my flashbacks. Of my panic attacks. Of being hit over the head again and again with the realization that my Noah was no longer on Earth. I was fucking terrified. And my body, my neck, my shoulders, especially, felt like steel. My stomach felt as if I were in a constant state of fear of falling, like that pit you get at the top of a roller coaster.

My life was shattered.

What I thought I knew about anything and everything was demolished. I had just experienced a magnitude 10 lifequake. That day, I died too. I didn't know how I was supposed to live. Or why.

I remember on the second or third day after he transitioned, I thought to myself, "Okay, this can't be undone. He chose this. And I have no other choice but to get on board." I knew that if I didn't accept what had happened, I would go insane. Begging and wishing for something to be the opposite of what it is—when there is nothing that can change it—is, in fact, insanity-making. I decided that I was Team Noah, in life and in death. If this was his path, I would have to get on board. I knew this was the hardest thing I would ever encounter in life, and I had no idea how to do it. The few things that could calm my insane mind and nervous system included reading about grief and the afterlife, listening to podcasts, and staring into space in the backyard.

I would swing between this knowing that I needed to accept this reality and the very real physiological grief expression that needed to take place. There were fits of grief where I just had to get out of my body. I would push, kick, scream, wail, grunt, curl into the tightest ball with every muscle contracted. And then, I would become so exhausted that I would lie motionless with a blank stare—as if I was dead. As I would slowly come out of that state, I would intentionally go to my altar for Noah and tell him how much I loved him and how grateful I was for our time together. I would desperately try to convey the depth of my love to him, hoping he was listening. I wanted him to understand what he meant to me, to us, to the world. I hoped he was watching me and listening to me. I wanted him to see the devastation he left behind, not as a punishment, but so he knew that his absence in this world was never something that would be "okay." So he could see how much he was loved and needed.

In those early weeks, I was seeing a therapist multiple times a week, and found that was about all I could handle doing. That and tending to Grant and Hope (Noah's siblings) as best as I could. As Noah's dad went back to work and the kids started back at

Noah and me in Thailand on a special one-on-one trip just seven months before he would leave this earth.

school (sort of), I was alone a good part of the day. And so, I began writing and sharing publicly. I wrote every day on social media as a dedication to Noah and my grief. I wrote to give Noah's friends bite-sized nuggets of wisdom to help them work through their own grief. To give my Earth-side kids a road map for their grief now and in the future. To share pictures of his beautiful life. I wrote with Noah by my side, often feeling him guiding what I wrote, and words flowed that I didn't even know I had inside of me.

I felt the need to share this grief. To allow others to share. To be witnessed. To allow me to connect without having to show my face in public and without having to interact. Eventually this writing replaced the need for the whiteboard. It calmed my mind. It helped me process. It helped me create intentional time every day to connect with Noah and my grief. To make sense of the world and life. And I honestly believe it has been a key factor in saving my life.

I've had this knowing come over me that Noah and I were supposed to be working together somehow. Initially, as I was writing and sharing, I did not have clarity on what that looked like, but it just dawned on me, right now as I'm writing the introduction, that these daily reflections, culminating in this book, were what we were working on together. This and likely many other things to come. Thank you, Noah.

I got to a point, on April 28, 2025, about nine months after Noah's transition, where I felt like I was beginning a new chapter in my healing. And so, I decided that it was time to get this *first* chapter out to the world. I have been told by those who have read my social media posts that they are relatable and give them pause, something to reflect on in their own lives. Many have said that it should be made into a book for others to use as a tool in working through their own life challenges. You don't have to have known Noah, me, or even to have lost someone to find value in following along on my journey of transformation. We each inevitably face our own lifequakes, and just being alive can be a challenge. *Noah Grants Hope* allows the reader to follow along on a healing journey, hopefully finding bits of themselves in my words. And maybe even finding nuggets of wisdom that resonate and inspire. This book is meant for those grieving the loss of a loved one, but also for anyone who has encountered struggles and other losses in life and wondered what this human life on Earth is all about.

A quick aside to understand the flow of the book: Each entry was originally a post on Instagram. I wrote every single day from September 2024 to April 2025, whether I had the energy or mental capacity to really express myself or not. As you read, you will see my process. My ups and downs. My insights. My questions. My intense feelings. Some days, I had one sentence of love to share. Some days I had long and potent reflections. Each entry was limited to no more than 2,200 characters on Instagram, which in hindsight I believe helped me to really get to the heart of what I was trying to understand for myself or to convey to others. As I transitioned these posts to entries in this book, sometimes I include pictures, and other times there may be references to pictures that intentionally aren't included. It is essentially my daily journal of post-traumatic growth. It's real, messy, raw, and beautiful. It is my process of awakening to our real mission here on Earth, which I'm positive continues to this day (even if you are reading this fifty years from now).

Month
3

September 9

My sweet boy, Noah, transitioned out of his physical body and back into the spirit world this summer. It has become clear to me that my purpose during my time on Earth is to help others (which in turn helps me) to not only survive a physical loss of a loved one but also to reimagine what our relationship with death looks like. To help those of us left on Earth to move from suffering, because we love to find ways we can continue to love, which will ultimately ease our suffering, and maybe even change the way we live while we're here. I am using my writing and reflections to document my journey as I discover how to continue living without him physically with me. Physical death is the only thing we 100 percent know will happen to us and those we love. We are not alone in this experience. My hope is that others moving through this same journey will find comfort, understanding, and community here.

September 10

My lifeline since Noah's transition to the spiritual realm has been to focus on how grateful I am for our time together on Earth and how much I loved him and will continue to love him. Trust me, this is not toxic positivity—I feel intense sadness, despair, sorrow, guilt, etc. I let those feelings wash over me, I cry, I feel numb—and then I focus on how insanely lucky I am to be connected to Noah. To know him. To love him. And to have his love. There is a choice in what we focus on in those moments of quiet after all of our emotions have spilled out of our hearts (and eyeballs). I can find those moments maybe just five seconds more each day. But I have to purposely make them happen with my intentional focus on love and gratitude.

September 11

I've heard the word *tragedy* quite a bit lately, so I want to share my thoughts on that word and its implication. Noah's life was a beautiful gift to his friends, family, and anyone who had the privilege of spending time with him. He was on Earth for a shorter time than most, and his departure leaves us feeling like we should have been able to do something to change the outcome. But to me, hardship in life, struggle, and death are just as much a natural and normal reality as ease, joy, and birth. Noah was meant to be on Earth for the nearly seventeen years he graced us with. He was ready to go home and move on to the next phase of his journey. This is a hard reality to accept because we miss him so much and can't stand the idea that he felt struggle or heartache. I had a thought pop into my brain recently that I feel like Noah implanted for me: What if we could look at Noah's transition as similar to sending a kid off to college? We are sad because we will miss their physical presence, but man, we are so happy for them as they move on to the next part of their journey that they have chosen for themselves. Their transition on to the next thing is not a tragedy. We celebrate it while at the same time mourn what we, ourselves, are losing. Can we celebrate all of the good work Noah did while in his physical body and also celebrate his return to the spirit world and the continuation of his journey? To me, this is how I continue to love Noah.

September 12

When someone dies, regardless of the reason, it's easy to go into problem-solving mode and try to figure out how it happened ... what went wrong, what could have saved them? This is especially true when someone takes their own life. This in turn creates guilt, blame, and suffering. It will not change the outcome. The hard reality is that the person in their physical form is gone, and our brains would rather feel guilt and suffering than not knowing or understanding. It's a natural instinct so that we can figure out how to not experience this pain again in the future. I have fallen into this trap, as I think many people in my situation have. My therapist asked if I could at a minimum say, "I did the best I could." I don't know if I can wrap my head around the best I had wasn't enough (an entirely separate post will come on our ultimate lack of control over an autonomous human and soul—which is terrifying). But what I can feel with 100 percent certainty is that I loved and continue to love Noah with all of my heart, with every cell in my body. I know literally nothing except for this. And focusing on that love can bring moments of peace and calm.

September 13

"We often believe grief will grow smaller in time. It doesn't. We must grow bigger." —David Kessler

I believe this to be true, and also like an impossible task at times. This is a marathon, to find meaning and peace that will last a lifetime. I did not prepare for this race and am struggling to breathe. I'm cramping up. I want it to end. But I do have hope that there will be a point at which a focus on meaning-making and living a life to honor Noah will feel possible. Where I can take a full breath, I can move my legs without them feeling like lead, and I can reciprocate the energy given to me by the supporters on the sidelines. Processing in a public way is the only way I'm capable of giving back in this moment, hoping that my words resonate and provide comfort and humanization of this most challenging process of trying to find a way back to living for others who have also experienced debilitating loss.

September 14

The fog rolls in and feels all encompassing at times. And as surely as it rolls in, it dissipates and the sun shines for a moment.

September 15

My sweet, sensitive Noah died from depression. His persistent depression didn't define him, but it was a constant struggle. One that he battled through adventure, travel, silliness, snowboarding, soccer, skating, friends, snuggles, sunshine, nature, and more recently therapy and medication. Noah's diagnosis was one that runs in his family. He came by it through no fault of his own. Why is it that we ignore or just consider it part of life when people who are struggling emotionally eat, drink, don't exercise, etc. to a point of organ failure and ultimately physical death? Why do we think that DNRs, pulling the plug, or physician-assisted suicide are all compassionate options for physical illness but not mental/emotional suffering? Why do we think that everyone who is experiencing depression is a "Stage 1 patient" with a variety of effective treatments that will eventually lead them to a life without consistent suffering? Why do we say someone who died from depression took their life when it had been taken from them the day they began suffering without an effective solution? There is help for most/many who experience depression. I am one of those people. Throughout my life I've been a Stage 1, 2, and 3 depression sufferer, especially when life gets challenging and lonely. But I see periods of light because therapy and environmental shifts work for me. If I was Stage 4, like Noah, these treatments likely wouldn't have helped. We lump people with mental health challenges (which I would venture to say is a large majority of the population) in to one category and lie to them and ourselves to offer a false sense of control if we think everyone can be helped. And, if they end up doing something to end their suffering, we think that *we* or *they* failed. We would never say that about a cancer patient. Noah tried. He didn't give up. He succumbed to his illness. And that is devastating for those left behind. It's time we change the narrative around death from depression. Everyone deserves compassion, love, and understanding, especially when they are dying. All I'll ever want for my baby is to be happy and free from suffering.

September 16

Part of me feels guilty when I experience anything that isn't intense sorrow, and part of me wants to continue feeling the depths of this profound loss even though it is torture when I allow those feelings to wash over me. If I keep feeling it, I can somehow keep holding on to Noah. I fear that if I begin to live life again, we will somehow be moving on without him. And I refuse to live a life without Noah. My logical brain knows that nothing I do or don't do will actually change the new reality that has been given to me. Where Noah is no longer physically here. And the inner knowing I have reminds me that time is an illusion, I am on Earth for a reason, and Noah is still alive and with me in spirit. This is the shift in thinking I attempt to spend more time in each day. To step out of the matrix to realize I'm in the matrix, and to sit in my knowing that I am a soul in a human body, not a human body with a soul. That I am connected to Noah's soul forever. That I can connect with him whenever I quiet my mind and allow him in. And I should be living the full human experience—pleasures and all—while I'm here. Dying from depression isn't selfish. Noah did not want suffering for anyone. In fact, that thought caused him great pain. We all have our own individual journeys—and for those that loved Noah, ours is to wade through grief and sorrow to find the light and love that is Noah.

September 17

Yesterday was my birthday. I could feel it was going to be easy to dive into a tailspin of despair as I imagine it will be at every special occasion. Normally, Noah would have written me a sweet, heartfelt handmade card. Birthday and Mother's Day cards are times he would express his feelings so sweetly and vulnerably through writing. I had no idea that Mother's Day of this year would be my last card from Noah. So, I had a choice to make yesterday morning when I opened my eyes and felt the heaviness of not having Noah with me physically. I could wallow and crawl into a little ball, shutting out the world, not knowing if this would be my last birthday with those I love who are still on Earth. Or I could try to show up as best as I could to share and accept the love from my precious humans that continue to be my source of love and light while I'm still here. I don't want to hold back creating memories and exchanging energy with my Earthly loves. What a waste of our short time together in this human form that would be! Noah encouraged me to step out into the water to find his gift for me yesterday. The most perfect red heart immediately caught my eye, and I knew it was from him.

September 18

"If love could have saved them, it would have." It wasn't about the love. That was never a question. Why is it so hard to accept the cycle of physical life and death? To lose the physical attachment to a loved one? We talk about attachment as a bad thing because it seems as though that is what causes suffering. Attachment to people, scenarios, ideas—when we can count on consistency, we feel safe. If we rely on something or someone that could leave us, we feel fear. But we are all connected, securely attached to each other as part of one big energy. It's the amnesia we have to our knowing of constant and consistent connectedness that creates suffering. It's the false idea that we have accepted as truth that it's possible to be all alone. That it's possible to lose connection with a soul when we can't physically see them or verbally communicate. How can we create a life in which we focus on this knowing to awaken ourselves and ease our suffering?

September 19

No words today. Just feeling the heart-bursting and simultaneously heartbreaking magnitude of my love for this beautiful soul.

September 20

Today I woke up happy for the first time since Noah transitioned nearly two months ago. He came to me in a dream last night and instead of the quick visits I've had with him in my dreams he stayed for a while this time. I have no doubt it was really him making an effort to comfort me. As I was lying in bed, reflecting on the dream, it came to me that everyone feels the need to say, "Nobody really knows what happens after we die." But don't we? Every person I have come in contact with who has lost someone has received a sign from them after they have passed. They might doubt it at first, but deep down they know it was a communication from the departed. There is so much documented and peer reviewed research on near-death experiences that tell us that there is life after death—this is not a made up phenomenon. Why do we feel the need to say that we don't "really" know just because we ourselves haven't died yet? We haven't been to the moon or the depths of the ocean, but we take others' words for it, accepting that the unbelievable and unimaginable are real. We see miracles every day and somehow can convince ourselves that they aren't miracles. They are just coincidences or luck or part of life that we have deemed as ordinary after seeing it so many times, like childbirth, sunsets, the moon's pull on tides. The more you open yourself up to seeing the magic, the more it becomes visible and the easier our departed loved ones can connect with us.

September 21

I'm realizing that the only way I can connect with Noah is by slowing down and being intentional about it. I am currently dealing with PTSD, and the other day, I was sitting outside, as I do nearly every morning. It's my time to be quiet and reflect on my thoughts and feelings about Noah's transition. I asked Noah why it had to happen this way, why it had to be so traumatic. I suddenly understood that if I didn't have this condition to deal with, I never would have slowed down to hear him, connect with him, and learn from this. I wouldn't have slowed down to figure out how I will continue Noah's legacy. I would have tried to get busy again to avoid this terrible pain and sorrow. But I can't get busy. My brain and nervous system are injured and won't let me. I am forced to be still. And I'm recognizing how important stillness is to begin to understand the big things in life. To see my path clearly. To continue to develop my relationship with Noah. To be there fully for my Earth-side kids and loved ones.

September 22

In the days after Noah's transition we were dealing with how to talk about what happened publicly, being asked by the school district and those helping to plan the service if we wanted the suicide hotline and links to resources put into official communications. I had a very strong reaction to this. While there is always a place for formal/institutional supports, no hotline or link would have saved Noah. It's a box to be checked by institutions to say they didn't ignore it. I did not want to be a part of this surface level and, in my opinion, inauthentic way of helping others who are experiencing this level of despair. I honestly don't know if Noah could have been saved, but I know with certainty that a link or a hotline to a stranger wasn't it. The term "suicide prevention" feels a bit offensive. "Know the signs" is bullshit. This simplifies a very complex and nuanced issue. Nothing is as easy as knowing the signs and having a number to call. We lean into this because we want to feel a sense of control, when in reality, we don't have the answers.

Some things can't be fixed. Some things require major changes way upstream, not at the last hour. Each person and situation is different. And it's terrifying to think we don't have a solution if we just see the signs and access the resources. I do know that caring, consistent, authentic, open, and vulnerable connections are a start to opening the conversation about our feelings, struggles, knowing we're not alone and that others experience struggles as well. I do know we need to expand and take the stigma out of the conversation around suffering, death, choosing to end a physical life, the importance of community and true connection. I do know that love and compassion go much further than a link or a hotline. And I do know that we can all be more mindful of intentionally providing both.

September 23

While we are all connected and here on Earth to help walk each other home, we are also all our own autonomous beings, working to make the best decisions for ourselves along the way. I have spent much of my life trying to control outcomes. Thinking I could save or somehow fix people I loved. There are many times I've had the crazy thought that I wish I could put my babies back in my belly where I know they would be safe and loved. Having a child is quite literally deciding to walk around the world for the rest of your life with your heart on the outside of your body—exposed and vulnerable to the weight of living in our society. Our children ultimately have to experience hardship and love from those outside of their parents in order to grow.

Our children come through us to go on their own soul journeys. They are not beholden or responsible for how their journey impacts us. They must honor their own path, and our work, as parents, is to love and support them along the way.

I am trying to find grace for myself in knowing I loved Noah unconditionally. I have and will continue to support him in whatever choices he makes for himself. Whatever he decides he needs, I am Team Noah. That is my job as his parent. To love and honor him as he moves through his own, unique soul journey.

September 24

Largely, in the Western world, death is seen as the worst, most horrible thing that could happen to a person. This assumes many things:

1. That death isn't supposed to happen.
2. That what happens after physical death is bad.
3. That physical death means they are gone forever and we will no longer be able to have a relationship with them.

What if we shifted the paradigm around physical death and recognized that:

1. Birth and death are both portals to the spiritual realm and our time on Earth is just a part of our existence and not the entirety of our being.
2. That we continue to have a relationship with our loved ones—we just have to shift into acceptance that the relationship now requires stillness, openness, and total presence to access.
3. That many humans die "prematurely" or "in a tragic manner." But these definitions are based on our view of death as bad. Just because someone returns to the spiritual world before they are 85, and didn't die in their sleep from natural causes, doesn't make their time on Earth any less meaningful or "what should have been."
4. Death is part of the grand design, just as the miracle of birth is. Both break the heart open to realize more love than you ever realized could be possible.
5. If we can stop trying to ignore or push away death, maybe we can start to accept and embrace it as the beautiful miracle it is, setting the soul free from the human body and this round of learning on Earth. Realizing that both our time on Earth and our time in-between lives is sacred, special, and should be honored.

How could this shift in perspective ease suffering for both those dying and those grieving? (I understand this perspective requires that you believe in an afterlife. If you question this, I encourage you to visit the Bigelow Institute to read physicians' award winning essays on their experiences that have proven to them that consciousness is separate from the human body.)

September 25

My initial reaction was "this isn't happening," "this isn't real," "I don't want this life," "I refuse to accept this life without him," "what did I do to deserve this," "I can't survive this." And then I realized, I don't really have a choice. I suppose I could lay in bed with the covers over me and slowly die from heartbreak, but then I would miss life with my other beautiful and amazing children. So, that has forced me to dig deep and figure out how I can possibly accept this new reality. It is the biggest challenge I've faced in life. Non-acceptance and resistance equals suffering. This is one of the few things I know. And it is one of the hardest things to do. It is taking up all of my mental and emotional energy … to be still, to find acceptance, to continue to love.

"Am I better off making up an alternate reality in my mind and then fighting with reality to make it be my way, or am I better off letting go of what I want and serving the same forces of reality that managed to create the entire perfection of the universe around me?" —Michael Singer

September 26

Excerpt from my Eulogy to Noah:

Several years ago, when we moved onto the boat we had an epiphany: that success is not what society tells us it is, but rather what makes us happy and brings us peace. This has been a core value for our family. We always told Noah that we would support him in any endeavor he wanted. Whatever path brought him joy and peace, we were Team Noah.

I had this conversation with him the last week of his life as he was struggling with a decision ... I told him, "No matter how I might feel about it, if it feels good and right for you, then I support you, and I am Team Noah." And if it doesn't and you don't want to do it, then I'm still Team Noah. I am ALWAYS Team Noah.

September 27

Excerpt from my eulogy to Noah:

Noah and I both have a critical thinking and maybe a little rebellious streak in us—we both don't think stupid rules should be followed. Last year we were working on getting to class on time. One day (as happened many, many days) I got a call from the school that he was tardy. I texted him and asked what was going on. He replied, "I was just playing hacky sack a lil." Even though he should have been in class, this made me laugh out loud. I asked him about it later, and he said it was a sunny day and he had nothing important to do in class. The parent in me had to lecture him, but the human in me admired his determination to live a life with as much joy as possible, regardless of societal expectations. And I think that is what Noah's last act was: an attempt to find peace and lightness even though it went against societal rules. And while that choice is devastating for those left behind, I am, and always will be Team Noah.

September 28

Excerpt from my Eulogy to Noah:

Noah was struggling, both with his physical body being able to support his active lifestyle and with his emotions. I want you to know that he was so brave as he tried to get a handle on both. He tried so hard to stay here with us. He struggled to communicate the depth of his pain.

As we move through our collective grief, I want to offer a lens through which we can try to find peace …

"Grief, I've learned, is really just love. It's all of the love you want to give, but cannot. All of that unspent love gathers in the corners of your eyes, the lump in your throat and in the hollow part of your chest. Grief is just love with no place to go." —Jamie Anderson

I encourage all of us to take that love for Noah and pour it into your friends, family, and community. Pour it into honoring his memory. Pour it into finding joy for yourself.

As we grieve the loss of our sweet and brave Noah, we may feel anger. I am angry that his physical body, brain chemistry, and his sweet and sensitive soul could not support a life of joy on this Earthly plane for my precious boy. But I will never be angry with Noah—I am Team Noah, forever.

September 29

There are days I can get by, but this past week I haven't been able to pull myself out of the overwhelming heartbreak. I sat outside watching the sunset last night—the sky was on fire. And I thought I'd happily never see a sunset again if it meant I could go back in time and erase what happened on July 25th, 2024. I thought, while certainly there is beauty and magic in the world, none of it means a thing without my sweet boy being a part of it. In a fit of grief, through sobs and a snotty nose, I told my partner that I hate this life. It's stupid and cruel and torture. And yes, there are good moments, but none of it is worth this pain. Not a sunset, not a laugh, not a beautiful forest—fuck it all. It's meaningless. I don't want it. I want my sweet boy back ... and if I can't have that, then I want nothing. And then I felt a quiet calmness come over me (Noah), and I thought about the immense amount of love I have for my children. My heart wants to explode when I think about it. There are no words to describe how I feel about them. And while this pain feels like it's literally breaking my heart into pieces and is physically and emotionally the hardest thing I've ever experienced, at the very same time my heart is exploding with love. If I had known this would be the outcome when I birthed Noah, I would do it all over again in a heartbeat. I would soak up every laugh, cuddle, talk, and adventure. Because, I guess, as it turns out, love is the one thing that makes the pain worth it. Somehow, my intense love for him and Grant and Hope is bigger than anything. Even the thing that feels like it's going to kill me.

September 30

It's time we change the conversation around suicide. And to start, we need a different term that's not so loaded. Those with mental health or physical health issues, who aren't part of the physician assisted death movement, don't get to have a compassionate term that isn't filled with judgment. They don't get to have the conversation about treatments, dead ends, and make decisions in partnership with their loved ones. They don't get to have the goodbyes, the closure. They don't get to save their loved ones from a traumatic surprise. They are not afforded a "good death." Their families are stripped of ever having real answers. Suicide is a leading cause of death in all age groups except the elderly, and this only accounts for those accurately reported.[1] It also does not include attempts that did not result in death, and it doesn't include those who have considered it but not attempted. This is a pervasive health concern. And as we have done for those with heart disease, cancer, diabetes, liver failure, and other major health concerns, we need to have open and honest conversations about treatment efficacy and options for those that are not responding to treatment and are suffering. I believe, if we were to have a society in which this is how we approached those who are suffering so much that they do not want to live, we would actually increase the chance of people communicating and working through all of the options and making informed decisions instead of decisions out of desperation and isolation. Imagine knowing that if you voiced your true feelings you may be locked up in treatment that potentially causes more trauma and suffering—that your freedom, autonomy, and ability to be a part of your treatment plan will be taken away. It's no wonder people are suffering in silence and making secret choices that hurt both themselves and their loved ones more than is ever necessary.

---

1. "Suicide," National Institute of Mental Health, last updated March 2025. https://www.nimh.nih.gov/health/statistics/suicide.

October 1

What is enough suffering? My favorite theory in my doctoral program was Social Construction of Reality. It posits that every single norm, rule, law, and way of being comes from society's creation of it. Nothing is inherently right or wrong—we, as a culture, *decide* it to be so. These norms evolve and change over time, and we often look back and think, "Wow, I can't believe we ever thought X, Y, or Z was okay!" We see how cultures all over the world see things differently, especially around death, dying, and grieving. Our society has deemed those with terminal physical illnesses, who are eighteen or older, and have an estimated six months or less to live as having suffered enough. What an interesting and arbitrary legal definition of who is allowed to choose a peaceful death! My hope is that we can start to create a new reality around assisted death. A new reality that includes being able to talk openly about our struggles and thoughts around not wanting to continue to live in suffering. About what role suffering plays in our lives and how we want to approach it. About acknowledging the real struggle of persistent depression and the mind-body connection when dealing with chronic physical pain. A reality in which we never have to wrestle with these thoughts alone, where it's as normal as discussing the treatment plan options for cancer.

October 2

Control is an illusion. Control over another's emotions, reaction, body, choices ... We like to think we have a solution for all of our human ails. If we just do "X," then it will be okay. We lose sight of the fact that we are all having our own, personal and unique human experiences. And while we can be helpers or hinderers, ultimately, nobody can make us feel better, see things a different way, accept love, etc. This is a harsh reality for those seeing a loved one suffering. I felt this with Noah and now those who love our family feel it with us. Not being able to save Noah, and now experiencing this grief that nobody can make better for me, I am intimately aware of the lack of control from both sides. So what do we do with this information? I think we just keep walking each other home. Being kind, compassionate, loving, and generous. And knowing that while it might ease the path or even provide optional alternative routes that might be better in our eyes, we must relinquish the facade of controlling another's autonomous path ... their experiences and lessons. As always, easier said than done, but something to consider that can ease our suffering.

October 3

My loves! My kids are not typical siblings. They are so sweet to each other. Kind, caring, and protective. So grateful for all of them and how they continue to care for each other. I'm one lucky mama to have these souls in my life.

October 4

Excerpt from my eulogy to Noah:

A dear friend gave us a message from Noah: While we grieve, feel regret, deep sadness, blame, shame, whatever it is … we need to know that we cannot find Noah there. While we will need to process and feel the full range of emotions for a while, we need to know that we can only find Noah in our joy, in our bravery, in our connection and vulnerability with others, in our love, in nature. That is where we can go to find and connect with our sweet boy. To my buddy, my sweet, sweet boy, I have loved you and will continue to love you with every fiber of my being. I will try my very best to be brave and thoughtful like you. And I will miss you so very deeply.

October 5

I would do anything ... I would have done anything ... I wailed this over and over to the altar I created for Noah in the weeks following his transition. And now I am feeling this very strongly about my Earth-side children. I will do anything to help them. The one peer resource for kids in Portland has a very, very long wait list. And peer support, community, and relating with those who "get it" is hugely important for healing. I feel Noah's guidance to create more opportunity for kids and families who are grieving to come together. This is why I keep writing and sharing.

October 6

Have you ever noticed that when you ruminate on a thought, looping it over and over again in your head, the emotion surrounding that thought gets bigger and bigger, too? And when you are vulnerable enough to say it out loud, often it seems a little smaller and less overwhelming? The power behind the thought is lessened? Or at least the pressure cooker inside your head and heart has lost a bit of steam? Having someone you can say your deep, dark thoughts to has so much power. The one thought we don't feel like we can say out loud is that we don't want to be alive. That the weight of it all is too much. And that we don't have hope for a better future. Imagine the weight that could be lifted if we created an environment where we could say this out loud and realize that we are far from alone. That this thought crosses a lot of minds. I'd like to challenge you to try to create and be that space for your loved ones. You are not alone in your human experience of pain and heartache.

October 7

Vulnerability—How can we truly connect with anybody without it? Being open and honest about life's joys and struggles is how we encourage others to do the same. And we find connections that may have been sitting right in front of us without even knowing it. I've received a lot of comments about how honest I'm being after Noah's passing. I think it happened because I want to model for my kids that we have nothing to be embarrassed or shameful about. That we have to be open and honest about our needs and struggles if we want to get any useful help. And that we have to get out of our own heads and hearts occasionally to look up and see others who are struggling as well. Of course we don't want to see others struggle, but there is so much power in shared experiences. While we need alone time to process, feel, and reflect, we also have to come together to heal and make meaning.

October 8

Suicide is the second leading cause of death for people ages ten to fourteen and twenty-five to thirty-four.[2] But services for those dealing with the grief associated with this loss are seemingly only for adults. When we experience a significant loss, it is life altering and has the potential to alter the trajectory of our lives in a way where we grow positively or change destructively. We have a unique opportunity to impact youth, who have little life experience, to help them through this grief. This period of intense grief is actually a window of opportunity to create a trajectory that is focused on personal growth instead of self-destruction.

2. "Suicide," National Institute of Mental Health, last updated March 2025, https://www.nimh.nih.gov/health/statistics/suicide.

October 9

The meaning of life ... I've been doing a lot of thinking about why we are here and what happens when we die—if I'm being honest, it's turned into an obsession. I'm reading, journaling, listening to podcasts, and having conversations in every spare moment I have. There is a school of thought that our time on Earth is to experience suffering so that we can fully know love. That we can never fully know the light until we have experienced the dark. I think there is some truth to this. But that then begs the question—is all suffering the same? If we take medications to ease suffering, are we thwarting our own growth? If the suffering feels like too much, is hitting the eject button on Earth eliminating that opportunity for growth? What suffering is the productive kind and what is just excessive? I've found in my own life that hardship has, in fact, made me a more thoughtful, passionate, and compassionate person. I've also had moments where it has felt like too much to bear. I've somehow made it through those times to find more light on the other side, but that is not everybody's experience. Especially those with chronic mental health and physical health issues. I am not claiming to know the purpose of life. Or the role ending one's life has in it. But it's worth wrestling with. And maybe if we wrestle with it out loud and together, we can at least find understanding, community, and love as a byproduct.

Month
4

October 10

Noah was often making funny and cute faces. This guy was good at making people laugh. We've heard from so many kids that Noah was always kind, genuine, and made them feel comfortable being themselves. We never know what someone is truly feeling as our internal worlds are known fully, only to us. Talking can let some of the steam out of the pressure cooker, but often we don't have the words to fully express our emotions and experiences. And no amount of talking can take away the pain. We can add all of the good things to our lives—laughter, connection, adventure, nature, love, touch—but we have to deal with the pain too. No amount of adding positive things can make up for or erase our struggle. And sometimes the pain is just too much to bear. My mission through *Noah Grants Hope* is to lead by example and create an environment where we can show and feel ourselves fully. To bear witness to others doing the same, without judgment or trying to control an outcome. We're in this life together. I see you.

October 11

No words today. Some days the reality of my new life without him kicks me in the gut, and I have nothing. Just deeply missing this funny, brave, sweet, sensitive boy's physical presence. I love you, Noah.

October 12

This sense that I got, just after Noah transitioned, of being in the matrix has not gone away. When I look at people, I see a little ball of soul energy bopping around in these weird, beautiful bodies that we have chosen to carry us through our journey on Earth. I haven't been able to bring myself to see Noah's body's ashes yet; it's just too real. And I had convinced myself that it didn't matter because he was not his body. While I still believe that to be true, I've been thinking about how our bodies are very special vessels that deserve to be honored for their role in our spiritual experience. We crave touch, snuggles, physical intimacy because it's as close as our soul energy can get while in human form. In my human brain, that is what I'm grieving—the loss of feeling connected to my boy while I'm still in my body. That knowing that we are connected because I can feel it physically. It's a huge transition and shift in thinking and perception to focus solely on our spiritual connection. But when I focus on what I can't just see with my human eyes or feel with my human body, I can feel and hear him so strongly. He imprints thoughts into my head, emotions into my heart, and I can feel his strong vibration and love surrounding me. Sometimes the sense of love is so much that it's overwhelming and brings me to my knees. I need this quiet time to feel him. I will protect it and make sure I have it everyday so I don't get sucked into the basic thought that we are only connected to those who we can see and touch.

October 13

Here are excerpts from the *Three Pillars of Zen* by Phillip Kapleau Roshi (Vintage, 1989) that Noah is encouraging me to meditate on lately:

All forms in their essential nature are empty. That is, mutually dependent patterns of energy in flux. Yet at the same time are possessed of a provisional or limited reality of time and space in much the same way the actions in a movie film have a reality in terms of the film, but otherwise are insubstantial and unreal.

Through zazen, the first vital truth is that all component things are ephemeral, never the same from one moment to the next, fleeting manifestations in a stream of ceaseless transformation, becomes a matter of direct personal experience.

We come to understand the concatenation of our thoughts, emotions, and moods. How they arise, momentarily flourish, and how they pass away. We come to know that this dying is the life of everything, just as the all consuming flame is the life of a candle.

That our sufferings are rooted in a selfish grasping and in fears and terrors that spring from our ignorance of the true nature of life and death becomes clear to anyone compelled by zazen to confront oneself nakedly. But zazen makes equally plain that what we term suffering is our evaluation of pain from which we stand apart. And pain when courageously accepted is a means to liberation in that it frees our natural sympathies and compassion even as it enables us to experience pleasure and joy in a new depth and purity. (p. 14-20)

October 14

Yesterday was the anniversary of Noah's due date. He really didn't want to come out and after three days of labor and bursting the capillaries in my eyes from pushing so hard, he arrived Earth-side on October 17th, 2007. When my dad and uncle died, anniversaries and birthdays never really got to me. It was the everyday that was hard. This loss has been different and harder in many ways. While my dad and uncle also had "untimely" deaths, I didn't carry them in my belly and watch them grow. They weren't physically a part of me. I didn't go through every struggle and triumph with them. I wasn't responsible for their wellbeing. The afternoon before Noah transitioned he sat across from me at the dining table, and I asked how he was. He looked at me kind of funny and said, "Fine, why are you asking?" I said in a sarcastic tone, "I don't know, I grew you in my belly, birthed you, nursed you, wiped your butt, and have taken care of you everyday—I guess I kind of care about you." I have been bracing myself for this week. This birthday is one I don't know how I'll get through. I'm giving myself permission to stay under the blankets in silence and solitude. Fully feeling my grief. The aching in my womb and heart.

October 15

"The loneliest moment in someone's life is when they are watching their whole world fall apart, and all they can do is stare blankly. It's not the shattering itself that breaks you—it's the silence that follows, the quiet space where you realize there's nothing left to salvage. And in that moment, you know that you'll never be the same again. You'll build something new, perhaps, but it will never be what you lost." —F. Scott Fitzgerald, The Great Gatsby

I know this feeling very well. When Noah transitioned, the world literally became high def and slow motion, and I knew in that moment my family's whole world was forever changed. Oddly, in the moments immediately following, when I was in shock, I was noticing which first responders were intentionally and mindfully caring for us, and which ones weren't ... and what a difference it made to be seen, touched, and talked to in a genuine and heartfelt manner. Connection matters, in my opinion, more than anything. More than rules, protocols, or bureaucratic boxes to be checked. It takes so little—just a mindful and intentional opening of the heart.

October 16

He had that funny picture-taking smile for years. My babies are so stinking cute and so loved. The best of the best. I am so grateful they are mine.

October 17

The joy of my life. Today is the day we celebrate the beginning of Noah's soul's journey on this Earth with me as his mom, Pat as his dad, and Grant and Hope as his siblings. The beginning of the next sixteen years of learning, loving, adventure, struggle, and bringing immense joy to others. I am so grateful that we chose each other in this life. It was the joy of my life to be his mom. We have a new relationship now, one where we are working together and I am learning from him. We are partners now instead of Earthly mother and son. I don't want to say this would have been his seventeenth birthday, because living in the "would haves" isn't real. Today he is in his full power, love and light, guiding us if we slow down, connect, and let him. Today we remember and are grateful for his time on Earth. I have been feeling the immense weight of grief and feeling like it's just not possible to bear it. And I was reminded that grief is another expression of love. Without it, we aren't connected to our loved one. Grief is the path to connection and full expression of love. So I am trying out a new perspective ... I love my grief. I want it to stay. I want to always feel the intensity and depth of my love for Noah. Physical death can't take that away from me.

October 18

This painting is a precious gift from my chosen family, friends of my uncle's from my dad's and uncle's hometown. When Noah was born, the first thing I said when I saw him was "Uncle Rod?!" They looked identical. Recently, as Noah was maturing, he was beginning to take on my dad's features. Noah didn't get to spend much time with him before Rod passed, and he never met my dad. I would always tell Noah how much they both would have loved him, what an amazing Grandpa and Great Uncle they would have been. I think Noah would have appreciated their no filter, genuine, and heartfelt approach to life. I have wondered if they are reunited now, causing trouble and creating laughter. I like to think they are. My three special guys. They all knew and gave unconditional love. So grateful to be connected to them. And to feel my grief and love for them.

October 19

I was upset with Noah on his birthday for not giving me a strong sign that he was with us. I had been in an extremely low mood the entire week, similar to the week just after he transitioned. Yesterday and today, I have been bombarded all day with texts from those he loved with amazing signs that they have seen. This was my own direct reminder from him that he's trying, but I can't see what he's trying to show me through tears and negative vibrations. He's using his messengers to try to help me see. I feel you, Noah. I know you are here with us. I love you.

October 20

This picture … Grant leaning on Noah and Noah's arm around Hope. There are many pictures like this. I not only grieve the loss of Noah for myself, but for his siblings. We intentionally had three children. We wanted to build our own close family unit. That was not something I grew up with, and so I really wanted that for my kids. Watching their relationships develop is/was the greatest joy of my life. This lifequake that we have all just experienced changes all of our relationships … none of us are the same.

Lifequakes have the potential to tear families apart or make them stronger and closer. I'm grateful that this has made us more open, communicative, affectionate, caring, and devoted. I also feel how we are all closer with Noah. Sharing how much we love and miss him many times a day. Expressing what he means to us. Asking him for help and guidance. Having meaningful and deep exchanges with him daily. My kids are fucking amazing. My ever-growing and deepening relationships with them are what keep me going.

October 21

I've been doing a lot of thinking about the deeper spiritual meaning of suicide and what we are supposed to learn from it.

My spiritual view is that there is a larger plan and something we are supposed to learn from each challenge that is thrown at us. Honestly, I hate this view, but I really don't think we come to Earth to experience intense suffering for nothing. Life does seem to be one intense challenge after another, and for many of us, at least enough joy and meaning to keep us going. And I hate to admit that I would not have taken the time to slow down, reflect, feel, and grow as I have without the traumas in my life.

Maybe some souls come to Earth to leave us in this way so we can be split wide open. So that we can deepen our empathy for those struggling to the point of not being able to stay here. To make an active and concerted effort to connect with others and make sure they know we care about and love them. To see that we all are truly one. We are in this together. Because we are all here, having unique, but similar Earthly challenges.

It can't be some random mistake when thousands upon thousands of people die this way every year. There has to be a reason this is something that is even a possibility on Earth. I know this is controversial—as is saying there is a larger reason for any of the atrocities that happen every day. But how can we continue to live on this Earth, amongst this pain, if we don't try to find meaning? The world I live in can't be meaningless.

October 22

Everyday I sit down to reflect and connect with Noah. I look through his pictures, and I think about what is most present in my heart that I want to share and make sense of in my own head. It is my daily devotion to honor how he impacted and continues to impact us. I feel Noah is often guiding what comes to mind. On several occasions I have written and written and then somehow my phone decides to erase what I wrote, the app closes out of nowhere, or it glitches and freezes, not allowing me to post. This has happened specifically on a post I have tried to share on at least four occasions. Its content is about how I inadvertently contributed to this outcome and the lessons I've learned. I think Noah doesn't like this thought. I'm not sure why, exactly, as I feel like it's good to examine things to do better in the future. But for now, I'm going to listen to him and just let that narrative go.

October 23

I recently heard this metaphor and it really resonated with me: Life is like the ocean. If we live at the surface and try to ride the intense waves, we'll get tossed around and have to fight for survival. The deeper we go, the more stillness, calm, and peace we find. Here is how I find this stillness: First, find the Earth energy supporting and grounding you. Then, find the breath. Feel it move through your entire body, head to toe. Then, go deeper still until you can feel your own soul energy living inside of your body. Buzzing. Feel your own vibration. Finally, feel how your energy is connected to the Earth and the ether. You are connected, held and secure in the depths of this infinite energy. In times of chaos, we can find peace here.

October 24

At the recent Franklin High School soccer celebration for Noah, one of the moms asked me if Noah really liked playing soccer. I laughed and said, "Noah didn't do anything he didn't want to do." If he was playing, it was because he enjoyed it. I didn't want it any other way. And I love that part of Noah—that he knew what he wanted and needed and honored that. He knew the importance of living his own life and journey and not living for everyone else. Sometimes honoring what you want and need can be misconstrued as being selfish if it doesn't align with what others want from you or for you. But Noah was far from selfish. He considered others and was always there for his friends and family. He was generous, thoughtful, and present when you needed him. I admire his balance of knowing what he needed and caring about and working to maintain his relationships. Relationships were the most important thing to Noah—friends and family. This last thing that he felt that he needed is a tough reality to accept and can be misconstrued as him not caring about those who he loved and who loved him. But, it is clear from his communication and actions while he was in his physical body, and now as spirit, that he loves and cares about us so deeply. I feel you, Noah. I see you. And I love you, too.

October 25

I have been a shell of my former self. Somebody said living while grieving is like drinking a soda without any fizz. It goes way beyond that for me. At first I noticed that my voice was monotone. There was no light in my eyes, a smile was not possible, my energy felt heavy, like I was hauling a ton of bricks under my skin.

There are now some days I can laugh about something or muster a smile. My voice has a little bit more inflection. I find I can only feel more like myself around people who have acknowledged the depth of my pain.

As things have changed since the initial shock, I've noticed that I still don't know who I am, who I want to be. I don't know how to even think about experiencing joy or pleasure. I don't have the spark inside that is "me." My body and brain are walking through the world, but I don't know where my soul has gone. Maybe off somewhere to find Noah. Some call this derealization or depersonalization. An out of body experience. Dissociating. But, I have come to the realization that my soul has truly fragmented, and much of it is gone. It can't stand the pain. This might be seen from the outside world as depression, but the traditional treatments for depression won't bring my soul back. I believe the only way to find my soul again is to get to a place where I feel safe in my body and brain. To not feel like I'm going to die when I think about this new life I've been given without my sweet boy. I'm trying to figure this out—how to get there. And the one thing I know is that I can't do it alone. We need community, vulnerability, and honesty about our suffering to know we are in this together. Our experiences of suffering, learning and living are not unique, they are universal.

October 26

My beautiful boy. I'm thinking a lot about connection today. Real, true, deep connection. And its relationship with depression and anxiety, something that plagues so many of us. Having community and safe, supportive environments to have fun and adventure with is important. But someone you connect with on many levels— emotional, intellectual, spiritual, physical—where you can show all parts of yourself to and count on to always be there for you, no matter what, is what can be our anchor during rough times. How do we cultivate more of that? Especially for youth?

October 27

There is a loneliness epidemic all around the world. The UK was one of the first to create a government council to address it. I just read this morning that South Korea is doing the same thing. We throw money at a problem to create formal resources for people to have paid visitors come to their homes, create a 24/7 call center and programs that encourage social interaction ... Does anyone else see how crazy that is? This feels similar to hotlines and links being given for those who are feeling suicidal. This is so very clearly not the answer, and yet governments are spending hundreds of millions of dollars on these resources. It's time we get real. We need to strip everything back to the basics. True connection. Love. Vulnerability. Seeing ourselves in everyone else. I made a list of the universal causes of suffering the other day, the things we all have in common. There are ten things I've identified. We might only experience a few in each lifetime, but they are universal struggles. Struggles, that when we feel alone in them can feel like too much to handle.

1. Death
2. Chronic physical illness/disability
3. Chronic mental illness/disability
4. Addiction (food, substances, porn, etc.)
5. Loneliness
6. Poverty
7. Violence/abuse (verbal and physical)
8. Natural disasters
9. Self-worth
10. Relationships ending (romantic or otherwise).

We all also share in joy and connection. Can we just get real and be with each other in this human reality? Let's stop with only showing the good in our lives. We can only truly connect if we see all of each other—the sorrows and the joys. Can we commit to being real with each other? To stripping away the bullshit and getting back to love and connection?

October 28

When we lose connection with our own soul, it logically follows that we lose connection with others. In his note to us, Noah said that he couldn't explain it, but he didn't belong on this Earth. While I don't know exactly what made Noah feel like that, I can relate. And I know this is not an uncommon thought for others who have taken this path. For me, when I see the masses scurrying around, placing so much importance on reaching their idea of "success," or feeling stressed about being on time, getting good grades, looking a certain way, getting into the right school, attaining the nicest house, etc. I feel very alone. And I can see they have disconnected from their soul. I don't relate to these values. And these values are what our society is based on. So, it can feel like a trap if you aren't in this same mindset. It can feel like you have to play along to get through life. But it actually hurts your heart and soul to try to fit into this very strange way of life. It makes you feel disconnected from yourself if you do try to play along. And it makes you feel disconnected from everyone else if you don't. I've been doing a lot of research and my own theorizing on suicide, and I believe I'm coming to the conclusion that when we lose sight of the larger meaning of life, it can feel very isolating, leading to suicide. And on the other side of the coin, when you do see there is so much more to life, but you feel trapped, this can also lead to suicide. So, what is the answer? What do we need to work on? I believe it's finding our way back as a society to prioritizing and focusing on the larger meaning of life: love and connection. And we have to start that with ourselves and our immediate connections. There will be a ripple effect.

October 29

I learned a new word yesterday: "Vilomah." It's a word to describe a parent who has lost a child. It is Sanskrit for "against the natural order." I find myself in a very uncomfortable moment in time. One where I feel the time that has passed in the fiber of my being, and I'm beginning to feel Noah spending more and more time away from this plane. I feel so scared of losing my connection with him. I feel scared to continue to live without him. And I feel scared not to. I still feel like this just isn't real. It can't be real that I will never touch, smell, or see him again. But I wake up and go to sleep to reminders of his absence everyday that make me feel nauseous and numb at the same time. If I'm not numb, I'm in excruciating and debilitating pain. I am always thinking about Noah, both the trauma of his death and the good memories. And in those moments, I laugh or smile—if for a moment I get distracted—my brain brings me back to him with a jolt. My only solace and my sole focus for my personal growth right now is to work on being able to continue my relationship with him. Continue to talk to him, hear him, and feel him in a different way. I do feel that in my grief, as everything else in the world has been stripped away, I am closer to spirit. I am more open. I can connect like never before. I don't want to lose that. And so, I must find the middle ground—where I can simultaneously stay in my grief and my intense, never dying love for Noah, to stay connected—and to figure out how to live on Earth and learn to feel joy again. Figuring out how to live in a way that truly honors Noah is challenging beyond measure. But it is the greatest gift to be given the opportunity to find my way back home before it's the end of my time on Earth. I love you Noah. I love you Grant. I love you Hope. You are my heart.

October 30

I am wearing my cloak of grief. I find comfort in its weight. I honor this time and am coming to see how necessary it is to honoring and continuing the love for my beautiful boy. As a society, we do not honor grief as the sacred moment in time that brings us to our knees. We try to figure out how to move forward and not feel the intensity that it brings. It is excruciating to remove the armor around our hearts and feel it all. We think if we do, we might die from the pain. My grief is a window of opportunity. A time when the veil has been lifted, and I can see clearly. When my heart and eyes are open like never before. I used to think that people ran to spirituality during times of grief because they were desperate to find relief. I now see that one purpose of death being a known and predictable occurrence in life is to receive reminders during our time on Earth of our birth from and connection to the spiritual realm. It gives us the opportunity to reset and remember that this is Earth school, that we are always connected, and that love is the only thing that matters. That love cannot die. It cannot be taken away. It is stronger than we can fathom. Death is part of life. Death can give new life. Death is a great teacher. I love my grief. I have never felt so deeply in my life. I have never stopped this much to reflect and connect. I had lost sight of the depth of love that I had and continue to have. My grief is a great gift.

October 31

This was one of our most favorite memories from the boat. Cumberland Island, Georgia. Wild horses, horseshoe crabs, and the kids made us a hot dog dinner on the boat. We felt like we were finally exploring nature after a long haul down the East Coast. No deep thoughts today. Just gratitude for the time I've been gifted with my loves.

November 1

I wonder when the tears will stop flowing so regularly and with such excruciating physical pain in my heart. Some days I get through my new daily routine and am actually so busy that I don't have a moment to feel or cry. Some days it doesn't matter if I'm in the middle of a restaurant, on a walk, or at an intersection, nothing can hold back the ugly, snotty, and raw emotions from escaping. Some days I have time, but am numb and just feel the "knowing" that something awful has happened in my gut, but my head is still saying it's not real. Some days I fear my tears. And some days, I see them as holy and cherish them.

"For the simple truth is that great loss is wasted if we do not use it, over time, to discover what lies beyond great loss." This is from the life-changing book I've been reading: *The Wild Edge of Sorrow* by Francis Weller (North Atlantic Books, 2015). I think it should be mandatory reading for everyone as it offers a framework to think about the purpose of our grief in life (not just death), and offers thoughts on how to alchemize that pain. This is a poem by Rabbi Chaim Stern included in that book:

'Tis a fearful thing
To love
What death can touch.
To love, to hope to dream,
And oh, to lose.
A thing for fools, this,
Love,
But a holy thing
To love what death can touch.

November 2

What gives me a sense of calm after a period of feeling the storm? Awe-inspiring nature. The ever-present magic of a Fibonacci spiral. Quantum physics. This feeling of intense love that every person on Earth feels. The inexplicable magic of the infinite universe. The concept of infinity. The predictable and natural cycle of life and transformation of energy. Gravity. Water. Fire. Earth. Air. Oceans and the sun. Ladybugs and whales. The universal power of music and sound. Stunning sunsets and sunrises. Cloud formations. We are a part of something much, much bigger than us. Infinitely bigger.

November 3

"Hold your sorrow to a degree of eloquence whereby everyone around you will be fed by your efforts to do so." —Stephen Jenkinson

Becoming skillful at digesting our grief makes us a source of reassurance and stability for the wider community."
—Francis Weller, The Wild Edge of Sorrow

Everything in my life has changed. And quite dramatically. Noah's transition has created a seismic shift in all aspects of my life. I have only recently had the mental space to contemplate what it is I'm supposed to be doing with this experience. I cannot waste this grief. It is a great gift and teacher. I know I need to use it to somehow engage with life more fully and authentically. I know I am supposed to be working hand-in-hand with Noah to do something to better humanity. I still don't fully know what that is. But for the time being, I believe, it is to be an example of how to dive deep into your own sorrow to figure out how to truly and deeply experience life on Earth. To not forget your own soul journey. To consciously live. I love you.

November 4

"Approaching sorrow, however, requires enormous psychic strength. For us to tolerate the rigors of engaging the images, emotions, memories, and dreams that arise in times of grief, we need to fortify our interior ground. This is done through developing a practice that we sustain over time. Any form will do—writing, drawing, meditation, prayer, dance, or something else—as long as we continue to show up and maintain our effort. A practice offers ballast, something to help us hold steady in difficult times. This deepens our capacity to hold the vulnerable emotions surrounding loss without being overwhelmed by them. Grief work is not passive: it implies an ongoing practice of deepening, attending and listening. It is an act of devotion, rooted in love and compassion." —Francis Weller, The Wild Edge of Sorrow

The standard bereavement leave is three days in the United States. We have a service immediately after someone dies, and then we move on to grieve alone when we allow ourselves the time and space to do that, which doesn't always happen. When worldwide or natural disaster tragedies are happening, we might stop for a minute reading the news headline to feel, but we have no real way to process our collective grief. Our society says we should do what needs to be done logistically and then get back to life. Work, errands, chores. We don't take the time to fully process, feel, reflect. And this is what causes long term depression, anxiety, and discontent. We are disconnecting from our souls. From our authentic feelings. And in doing so, we disconnect from each other—maybe not superficially, but deeply. Part of that is because we don't have rituals in place to honor our grief and love. Part of it is because we are afraid to go there. Part of it is our culture's need to be its definition of "strong." We don't know the path to feel and process and come back out of it lighter and more authentically engaged instead of getting lost in the heaviness. We don't have this as a part of our regular life and routine. How much full, rich, authentic life and connection are we missing out on by not fully acknowledging and processing our grief? How much love can we not access because we don't know the depths of our capacity to feel?

November 5

"Grief is essential to finding and maintaining a feeling of emotional intimacy with life, with one another, and with our own soul. May you find nourishment in these pages for your soul and your commitment to stay connected to the course of life." —Francis Weller

As I go through pictures of Noah and revisit his distinct phases of life, I realize that there is grief in knowing I'll never see the newborn Noah again, the toddler, the seven-year-old, the preteen, the teenager. That would have been the case whether he transitioned to spirit form at sixteen, thirty, or seventy-five. Nothing stays the same. Life is ever-changing. And unless we are perfectly skilled at accepting non-permanence, we feel some level of grief or sorrow when there is change in any capacity in our lives—work, friends, hometown, ages and phases with family, etc. I think the work is to get as close to acceptance of non-permanence as possible. To flow instead of fight. To trust in the wisdom of the Universe. And we have to acknowledge the grief, feel it, and let it go. It can't be ignored. That is no small feat. It requires attention, devotion, stillness, and a trust in something larger than yourself and the knowing that while energy changes shape and form constantly, it never ceases to exist and we never cease to be connected to it.

November 6

Grief comes in my forms. Anticipatory grief is when you know a loss will be happening in the near future, and you can't ignore that reality in the present. You have no control over the outcome. Many are feeling that collective grief today after the election. I hope we don't turn back to our day-to-day busyness and shove those feelings away. Forgetting our outrage and sorrow or stuffing it away to get through the days. I do hope that we can largely stay in the present, keeping this longing for compassion, connection, and goodness in the world. And I hope keeping what we want to cultivate in our society everyday close to our mind and hearts makes a difference in what we CAN control, and that is how we show up in the world for ourselves, friends, family and larger community. It makes a bigger difference than we might think. The ripple effect is real. Also … just a friendly reminder that we're living in the Earth school matrix and what even is reality?

November 7

*"The collective denial of our underlying emotional life has contributed
to an array of troubles and symptoms. What is often diagnosed as
depression is actually low grade chronic grief locked into the psyche,
complete with the ancillary ingredients of shame and despair.
Martin Prechtel calls this the gray-sky culture. One in which we do
not choose to live an exuberant life, filled with the wonder of the
world and the beauty of day to day existence, one in which we do
not welcome the sorrow that comes with the inevitable losses that
accompany us on our walk here. This refusal to enter the depths has
shrunk the visible horizon for many of us, dimmed our participation
in the joys and sorrows of the world. We suffer from what I call
premature death—we turn away from life and are ambivalent
toward the world, neither in it nor out of it, lacking a commitment
to fully say yes to life." —Francis Weller,* The Wild Edge of Sorrow

Raise your hand if you feel caught in the hamster wheel,
overwhelmed, feel like we don't have time to truly connect,
depressed, anxious, or unfulfilled. I would venture to say most of
us have at least had long periods of time when we've experienced
this, if we're not also currently experiencing this. We're on autopilot
and disengaged from ourselves and others on a deep emotional
level. We are surviving, but not having a meaningful soul experience
on Earth. Weller calls this premature death. It's when the soul
part of us is no longer present, but our minds and bodies are. Eat,
sleep, work, entertainment. Repeat. I believe a radical shift in
how we engage in society needs to take place to allow ourselves
the room to create space for our soul experience, but baby steps
can be setting aside just fifteen minutes a day to connect with
ourselves. And fifteen minutes to think about and connect with
others meaningfully. Every day. As a devotion to life. To be real with
ourselves and others. Consciously avoiding platitudes or surface
level talk. Mindfully being vulnerable to foster deep connection.

The term *self-care* has been used for how we deal with stress/depression/anxiety, but my definition of that is making time to truly connect with yourself, others, and something greater than you. Not just finding relaxation or a temporary reprieve. This is what will truly make a difference in our mental and emotional health. This is what life is supposed to be about.

November 8

Recently, I've been talking with my other son about how we can approach our grief. This sorrow that feels like it's been dumped all over us. Did Noah do this to us? Or did he take a path of his own and we are left to figure out what our path will be? Free will comes from both directions—what we actively decide for ourselves *and* our responses to actions from our connection to others that impact us. From my vantage point we have three options:

1. We can allow grief to destroy us. Self-medicating, engaging in risky behaviors, or living in anger or despair that matches the depth of our hurt.

2. We can actively choose the passive life ... premature death, disengaging from deep introspection or connection. Protecting our hearts from feeling our past, present, or possible future pain. Apathy, depression, anxiety. But in turn, stifling our opportunity for soul growth as well as authentic joy and pleasure. Or

3. We can be conscious enough to choose to feel it all. To take the depths of pain and use that to become more empathetic, compassionate, loving, and present. To use these universal sufferings as the strategically built-in opportunities in Earth school that they are, opportunities for expansion and growth, knowing that feeling to the depths is beautiful and excruciating at the same time. I choose consciousness. Being real. Feeling. Depth. Connection. Love. I'm here for the soul revolution. Let's get back to living our lives consciously and on purpose.

I love you.

November 9

Boundaries. There is a big push in the mental health world to help clients set and maintain boundaries. I saw this boundary chart on a mental health care Instagram account the other day and I had a very strong reaction. It illustrated to me how this frame of mind is being taken too far, and is actually detrimental to mental health (aka soul health). We are advised to set boundaries in all areas of our lives in order to protect our mental health. It's so painfully obvious to me that we are missing the boat. What causes depression? And suicide? Not just the thing that happened. Because we all have these universal sufferings to experience in Earth school. But deeper than that. It is a lack of connection and love. It is feeling alone. It's not being real with each other. Suicide does not happen because of a mental illness (which is a social construct, by the way, as we need to dive deeper into what "mental illness" actually means). It happens because we lose sight of the fact that we are not alone. Our ego forgets that we are more than a human body and brain. Boundaries are the opposite of connection. Individualism is the opposite of connection. Ego is the opposite of connection. We, of course, need to show ourselves love and protection as we are part of the larger whole. But instead of focusing on all of the various ways we can create boundaries, should the focus not be on thinking about and cultivating all of the ways in which we can connect, love, and support each other? In a real, deep way. On the soul level. Let's set an intention to stop spending so much time in our heads and get back to our hearts.

Month
5

November 10

Today, I am tired. So tired of surviving each moment. It's exhausting. A new friend who has experienced this loss likened it to contractions. They come in waves and when you're in them you don't think you can get through them, but you know you don't have a choice. And during a moment of reprieve you are so tired and, at the same time, gripping, waiting for the next round that you know is right around the corner. There is no way around them, you must go through them. Ouch. It hurts everywhere. It hurts even though I know he's right here beside me when I call him. Even though I know he's okay. Even though I know I will see him again. It hurts in a way no words can describe. I love you.

November 11

I will be posting more about this as I have time to refine the synthesis of my research, but for now I just want to remind every parent out there that while one in four teens is depressed, antidepressants are contraindicated for youth unless the benefit of the medication outweighs the known risk of increased suicide risk from the antidepressant. Please do your own research before you agree to giving your child an antidepressant. Do not rely on a doctor's recommendation. Google the medication name and suicide risk. Know what aspects increase the risk. Educate yourself. Antidepressant use has skyrocketed over the last twenty years and so has the suicide rate associated with them. Especially for youth. I don't want this to feel like a fear-based message. I want everyone to feel empowered to protect their kids by being as informed as possible. I can't go back in time, but I can try to help in the present. I love you.

November 12

I recently heard that "the world is not ours to save." I know on a spiritual level this is true, and at the same time I am having trouble with this. It is so hard to see the injustices that harm so many, to see people going through life and not lifting their eyes to see what's going on. I want to shake everyone. Wake them up. Have fellow souls working together, hand-in-hand to make change. Big change. Change that makes the world better. Not to be indifferent or just shrug our shoulders thinking that the change that needs to happen is just too big. And at the same time, it feels daunting and exhausting just thinking about how to change systems that have so much power. I do believe in making change in our own little circles and the power of the ripple effect. But when it comes to life and death, I'm feeling like it has to be bigger. I will be relying on Noah's guidance to lead me in the direction in which I can make the greatest change. He is helping me to be as real as possible, own my voice and make it heard in an effective way. I love you.

November 13

I have been feeling somewhat alone as I realize all of the ways in which our society needs to change. I know I'm not actually alone. There are other people who have the same realization as me, but they just aren't that easy to find. I know for myself, the only time in my life that I've felt shaken up enough to re-evaluate everything, to change my priorities and way of being in the world, is when something Earth-shattering has happened. I've been feeling sorry for those that were close to me before Noah transitioned because I am not the same person that they knew. But I think I'm coming to realize that they are fortunate to be privy to soul-shattering change and growth without having to experience it for themselves. That maybe bearing witness to me finding my way out of the brokenness has value and can help others prepare for when they will inevitably have a great loss. Because that is life. Loss, joy, heartache, and love. And we just have to figure out how to utilize it for as much growth and expansion as possible.

November 14

"But don't we have enough pain of our own without taking on the pain of others? Herein lies the grand illusion for there is no such thing as 'pain of our own.' The only private pain is the pain of isolation, which is hell. All other suffering is communal. Like love, it can only be shared. If we are to share people's joy, we must also share their sorrows. Shrinking from sorrow, we shrink from joy as well." —Mike Mason

My friend posted this reminder the other day and it hit the nail on the head. I haven't been able to articulate why it's hard for me to be around people right now who don't know or haven't acknowledged the depth of pain my family is experiencing. Be with me in my pain so we can truly be together in joy. I will be with you in your pain and your joy. Because we are not separate. Your pain is my pain. Your joy is my joy. Be real with your soul, so you can be real with mine. I love you.

November 15

In the days and weeks after Noah passed, I made myself come to the conclusion that I had to accept and support him in this decision he made for himself. I want to believe that he really thought about it and knew what he needed. If that was the case I could try to get behind it because a mother just wants her baby to be happy. Now that I'm finding out he was given a medication that not only isn't FDA approved for those under eighteen because of increased suicide risk but that it also increases suicide risk to 4 percent of users (double that of the placebo), I realize that a doctor basically gave me a hundred-chamber gun with four bullets to give to my kid. And the empty chambers "might" help him with depression. This is a very hard thing to comprehend. I've been hearing the term righteous indignation a few times of late and relate to this feeling. It is not a good one as it takes up all the space in my head and heart. My son died, and it is very clear that drug companies are making money off of drugs that are dangerous, where four out of one hundred people risk death.[3] I am outraged and also don't have the energy to fight when I am grieving, which is what they count on. I don't want to come across as the crazy, bereaved mother that is just trying to point a finger—this is a real issue. I have these passionate feelings not because I think someone has to pay, but because I can't imagine another family going through this if something can be done to stop it. I don't think I could live with myself if I didn't try to make some large scale change. For now, I realize the way I can do that without losing myself in anger—and to continue to focus

---

3. Tyra Lagerberg et al, "Selective serotonin reuptake inhibitors and suicidal behaviour: a population-based cohort study," *Neuropsychopharmacology* 47, 817–823 (2021), https://doi.org/10.1038/s41386-021-01179-z; "Suicidality in Children and Adolescents Being Treated With Antidepressant Medications," US Food & Drug Administration, last updated February 5, 2018, https://www.fda.gov/drugs/postmarket-drug-safety-information-patients-and-providers/suicidality-children-and-adolescents-being-treated-antidepressant-medications.

on love—is through education on antidepressant use and through the creation of something that addresses the underlying causes of why people seek help from antidepressants in the first place. My mission is becoming more clear. Energy will shift. The tide will turn. Love wins.

November 16

To be human is to learn how to connect the head (the human part) and the heart (the soul). Not letting one take over, but melding the two to live our fullest expression of life, which is our fullest expression of love. What does that look like? I think it's different for each person. It's essential to figure out so we use our time on Earth to the fullest. This understanding of ourselves is our "Soul Work." For me, I've known since I was little that my fullest expression of love, where I can feel my heart expanding, is through advocacy, education, and being a voice for those who are marginalized. This boy and I had a special bond. He brought so much light into the world. I will take the light he has gifted me with and do this work in partnership with him. Expanding into the light and being conscious of not contracting in the darkness of the fight. Fiercely and passionately spreading love, education, and connection as a means to take out the darkness. My love for Noah, my family, and my soul community fuels my Earthly work. I'm eager to get to work with people whose mission aligns with my mission. Let's get to work. In community. As a team.

November 17

Pharmaceutical companies that sell antidepressants associated with increased suicide risk say that patients should just be closely monitored for signs. Do you know that knowing the "signs" isn't actually an evidenced-based prevention strategy? Identifying that someone is struggling emotionally and getting them help (this does not mean medication as has been put into our heads as the "solution"), opening the lines of communication, etc. is always a good idea. But it's most effective before someone is feeling suicidal—not after. The majority of people who are having suicidal thoughts do not tell you when asked. Why? They are already in a state of mind where they think they are a burden, they are beyond help, they don't see other options for themselves, they don't want to worry anyone, they don't want to be locked up or reported ... the list goes on and on. Putting someone on a drug that can increase suicide risk, and saying you will "keep a close eye on the signs," is not actually a strategy to prevent suicide. Prevention is getting to the root cause of depression. Prevention is true community. Prevention is connection. Prevention is vulnerability. Prevention is creating space for honest communication. Prevention is making space for grief. Prevention is a safety net. Prevention is prioritizing connection to purpose. Prevention is acknowledging and talking about from a very young age that we all have feelings of not wanting to be here or it being too hard. Prevention is doing Soul Work. Prevention is getting real as a community. Prevention is not medication that doesn't address the root cause, and it is not "knowing the signs." I love you.

November 18

I like knowing I can call on my spirit family when life feels like too much or I could use a little extra support. I have read that our spirit family is as close as our next breath. It's up to us if we engage with them. It's easy to forget this in the hustle and bustle of life. I have definitely forgotten this after my dad's and uncle's passing. I have forgotten that I can talk to them whenever I want—and they likely have better insight for me than when they were in their bodies. I call on Noah for help, but also for company. The ache of missing him is in my heart, stomach, and throat everyday. And when I can stop to connect with him it softens that ache. I've made it a daily ritual to connect with him. This is my grounding, my own "soul check-in," and helps me to not lose sight of what is important. Today, my sweet Grant is having surgery. I have talked to Noah and my spirit family to ask for their presence and comforting energy. I know Noah will be at his side today.

November 19

With suicide being the eleventh leading cause of death among all age groups, one could say that it is as "predictable" or "normal" as cancer or heart disease.[4] There are many different types/causes of suicide, yet we treat them all the same. Suicide is a general term, where chronic physical pain, chronic emotional/mental pain, terminal illness, depression, PTSD, lack of a safety net when the financial or emotional world gets ripped out from under you, the hopelessness of incarceration, anti-depressant induced suicidality, etc. are all so different. As different as breast cancer is from pancreatic cancer. And as different as Stage 1 is from Stage 4. Some are preventable. Some are not. Some are an ending to long-term suffering, some are impulsive. Some existing struggles are exacerbated by drugs (legal, illegal, and prescribed). They all feel excruciating to those left behind. I've done a lot of analyzing, and I've concluded that we need to treat these various scenarios as the unique contributors to suicide that they are and develop prevention strategies that are curated and dialed in. The challenge is that many are related to our current social structure. While changing the social structure takes time and can feel impossible at times, we can try to make a difference in how we, as individuals, respond to the social structure. We can benefit all scenarios from open and honest communication, real/vulnerable connections, and a connection to something bigger than ourselves. The same can be said for how those left behind learn to live again, regardless of the scenario.

---

4. Sally C. Curtin, Betzaida Tejada-Vera, and Brigham A. Bastian, "Deaths: Leading Causes for 2020," NCHS National Vital Statistics Reports 72, no. 13 (2023), https://stacks.cdc.gov/view/cdc/133059/cdc_133059_DS1.pdf.

November 20

We all know this, but sometimes it's helpful to have a reminder: In the game of life, there will always be a struggle or challenge. The name of the game is not to change the game, but to change our reaction to it. We can't change the external world (challenges we all need to work through), but we can change ourselves within it. We can grow from our challenges. This is called Post Traumatic Growth (PTG). And in my opinion PTG is the whole point of life. That and of course love—for ourselves, each other, and the Earth. I love you.

November 21

These two would meet in the hallway between their rooms after I tucked them in. When they were young and I was exhausted at the end of the day, it would frustrate me, and now I look back and absolutely adore their desire to be with

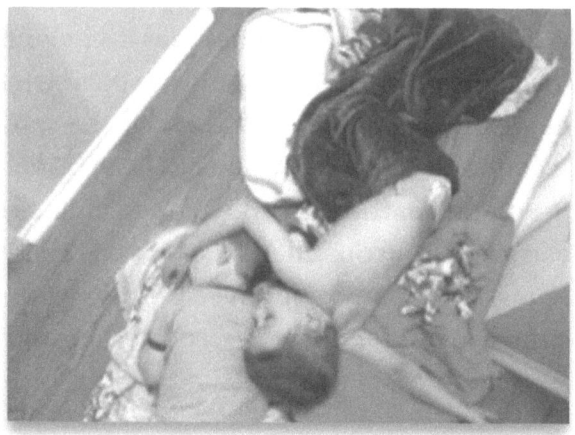

each other. This is one of my favorite pictures. I observed a mom at a coffee shop the other day—she was berating her young son about not "using his brain" when he put something in his pocket and then lost it. She went on and on, and the boy sat there with his head down. It hurt my heart to witness, partially because I wanted to scream to her that she should be kind and loving and gentle. She's lost sight of how precious each moment is and how much of an impact our words and actions have on our children. And partially because I know I had moments like that too, when I felt so overwhelmed with life that I lost sight of what's really important. It's not the lost toy. I can tell you that for damn sure. But those little things can so easily seem important.

Some might find it morbid, but I appreciate the exercise of writing your own obituary. Will it be focused on the least amount of toys lost, the most amount of money gained, the most timely to school, the least messy house, the most obedient children ... or will it be overwhelmingly the impact you had on your loved ones and community through your show of love? We are human. We will err. We will show our shortcomings and hopefully learn from them. But can we consistently, each day, bring ourselves back to what we want to be remembered for if we died tomorrow?

November 22

I often look at the dining table and picture him sitting there with us. Or hanging on the couch. My brain still hasn't quite accepted this massive shift in our reality. I'm about to head out to an early Thanksgiving celebration with my boyfriend's friends. The second social outing I've had since Noah passed. The first one ended with me leaving early and having a crying/panic attack in the parking lot. I'll be attempting to engage with people I don't know very well, some who know about Noah and some who don't. I'm sure I'll be asked the generic, how's life? What's new? Do you have kids? This is quite literally my nightmare. I can smile on the outside and internally feel like I'm going to die. I'm not very good at faking it. I can't lie and say, "I'm good." I have my standard, "I'm hanging in there" phrase. That one at least seems to be somewhat honest but doesn't make anyone too uncomfortable or ruin their good time. I suppose I could stay home. And maybe that would be best. But I don't actually want to be a hermit. I used to be social. I don't know how you start to live life again. At some point those conversations have to happen. And I suppose I should get used to saying I have three kids, one has passed, instead of avoiding conversations where I have to admit that to the world. It makes it more real every time I say it. Before I leave tonight I'll be reminding myself that everyone has something going on in their life that's a challenge. That I'm not the only one. I'm not alone. To be real. And to be soft with myself and honor my limits as I adjust to this new life. The holidays are a hard time for many. I challenge you to have real conversations this holiday party season. Have fun, joke … but also go deep and attempt to foster genuine connection. I love you.

November 23

I recently saw a discussion about the relationship between authenticity and grief. Grief rips you wide open. It makes all of the stupid, mundane bullshit crumble and become insignificant. You see life and people for what they are. There is no room for placating, faking, or spending what little energy we have in the midst of grief on insignificant things. Grief demands authenticity. I have been through losses before Noah and experienced the same thing. But slowly, as I was able to function again, I began to forget and became more and more beholden to what society expected of me again. My vision was clouded with the bullshit, and I lost sight of the authentic me. The me that does what feels good in my heart and gut despite the challenges or expectations put in my way. I'm dedicated to not losing the authenticity that I've found under the pile of shit that has fallen to the wayside from this seismic loss. Noah changed my life when I became his mom, and he changed my life when he became my angel. An emergence of new life and pure loving energy resulted from both his entrance and his exit from the physical plane. I love you, sweet boy. Thank you for everything you have given me.

November 24

The term self-care seems a bit shallow to me now. It's been conflated with doing things to bring ease "in the moment" of stress, but largely is not addressing the root cause of our unrest. I built a business on self-care. When I went to massage school, I realized that massage is basically induced meditation, but only if we remind the mind of what the body is feeling, use breath work, and guide it into a visualized meditation. That time can easily be lost with the mind thinking about what stressed it out before walking in the door, the groceries needed on the way home, etc. I saw an opportunity to make that time on the massage table work for us in a deeper way. That mind-body connection time is so important daily, and so we created a way to deliver that in a small group setting—making it more affordable and accessible. And it just happened to include community. Something we quickly realized was a huge part of why people loved it and felt better after a session. I see now how this regular connection of mind and body is the first step in building a foundation to address the root cause of our suffering. But we must also go deeper. To know and understand our own souls. To deeply connect with other souls. And to understand our place in the larger Universe. We must continually and ritualistically make time for stillness. To enter a meditative state. And to open our minds and hearts to what comes from that state of connection. To connect with and really hear what our souls are trying to tell us. And then to read. To discuss. To make art. To listen to music. To integrate what comes to us from this intentional, attentive and receptive stillness. The missing link is the going deeper in ourselves, with our community, and with the Universe. Daily. So that we do not get swept away with the pushes and pulls of our human lives and forget that we are souls in a human body. That is true self-care. I love you.

November 25

I read a parable about a grieving mom stuck in a hole—people passed by giving her suggestions, tools, listening to her vent about her struggle, suggesting medication to deal with the distress, etc. But she couldn't seem to get herself out of the hole. Then another mother who had been in the hole before threw a rope down and climbed into the hole with her. She had been there and knew how to get out. This really stuck with me. When we have been through something, I think it's our sacred duty to get into the muck with those that come behind us. Share in each other's sorrow and struggle, and share in the strength and hope required to continue to live. This special connection—feeling seen, heard, and understood—is critical to our human experience. It requires openness, generosity of energy, and vulnerability from both the one that came before and the newcomer. I will whole heartedly climb down in the hole and help you find your way out with anyone who wants me there. When we help others we are helping ourselves at the same time. We are one. I love you.

November 26

Today, I spent the day with a fellow mom whose son has transitioned. She wrote a book entitled *Together Forever*. This book appeared on my doorstep in the first days after Noah transitioned, gifted by a fellow mom who I did not know, but her son knew Noah. It turned out to be my lifeline. A different take on grief, she focused on acceptance and how to continue to foster a relationship with souls who have transitioned. She was and continues to be a beacon of hope for me. I feel lucky and grateful to now call her a friend. She is as real as they get. I have met so many wonderful people because of Noah's passing. It's weird and beautiful how grief and loss can bring people together as much as joy. I love you.

November 27

Duality and non-duality.

These are words spoken in spiritual teachings, but really just refer to being human in our mind's experience of opposing sensations: emotions like sorrow and joy, excitement and terror, that we are all separate beings (duality). And our soul's knowing that we just "are." We are one. We are love (non-duality).

Noah felt an emptiness and also a love for many things ... going to the mountain with his friends being one of them. He felt this duality. This separateness. I'm guessing separateness from his soul, from others, and from something greater.

In our quest on Earth as souls having a human experience, we feel unsettled living in duality, because we know it doesn't sit quite right in our gut. We search for our origin and purpose through religion, spiritual teachings, etc. And across many teachings—the constant is that we are one. That there is no duality.

This non-dualistic knowing eases suffering.

Today I felt excited for the first time since Noah transitioned. I felt excited about my path forward, working with Noah to make the world a better place as my path is slowly being revealed to me. And then, minutes later I went to therapy and continued to process my trauma ... feeling excruciating pain and terror. Duality.

It is a great challenge to be living the human experience and also live in non-duality. But it is the only way I know to ease my suffering. This is the most important work, as I see it. This is as real as it gets.

November 28

I've been feeling like I might be done posting old photos of Noah and our family. It pulls at my heart in gratitude for those times, but also with a longing for the past. I'm feeling called to have pictures of Noah around me as he is now. In the present. The signs I receive. The times I'm in nature when I feel him around me. He's so much bigger now than his soul contained in his human body. I am grateful he is in his full light and power. Peaceful and full of love. And I am grateful he continues to be in my life. Someone recently shared their observation that they think more about their departed loved ones than their family members that don't live near them. And they thought that perhaps that is because our departed loved ones are present and involved in our lives so much more than some of our living people. I feel that. I feel Noah so close to me every day. We are closer now than when he was alive. Today I am immensely grateful for my past ... the beautiful memories I have with my family. My present ... Noah's loving spirit, my beautiful living children, and the closeness that has developed over these past several months, our sweet therapy dog, Mia, my ever patient and loving boyfriend, old friends and new friends, an amazing therapist, my energy healer. And to my surprise, my capacity for love and my ability to continue to expand and grow in the midst of great sorrow. I love you.

November 29

My goal is to be in a high enough vibration where I can find my sweet angel. Where I can feel him, hear him, and connect with him.

I've heard over and over that spirit is as close as your breath. Our brain has a filter that doesn't ordinarily allow us to engage with those in the next dimension. But if we can strip away that filter and open our senses, we can connect. It is possible.

This requires stillness. It requires a focus on gratitude and love. An opening of the heart. A quieting of the mind.

As a mental health professional myself, I frantically tried to engage with all of the traditional mental health resources to help myself and my family after Noah transitioned. I was out of my mind and in so much agony, I was desperate for help. And yet I knew in my gut that no amount of talk therapy would make a dent in this. I did not want medication to take away any of it either—I wanted to feel the depth of my love (aka grief) for Noah, but I needed help wading through it, understanding it, seeing paths of others who had made it through the gripping darkness. To know that this wasn't actually going to kill me because the pain felt in the heart, mind, and body combined is pretty convincing that there is no way out.

I have found that my road out of the unbearable pain includes two main avenues ...

1. To begin to understand what the meaning of life is to me. What role death plays in life. To have a firm grip on what happens after our bodies die. To understand that we can still connect with our loved ones on the other side of the veil. To know it's possible to remove the human filter and see other souls, as well as our time on Earth, our connection, as so much more than our human minds reduce them to.

2. To know that others have walked before me, others walk beside me, others will continue to walk behind me ... and to feel a solid knowing that I am not alone. I am not alone with

the other humans next to me. And I am not alone with those on the other side as they are as close as my breath.

I am calling this Soul Work. It's my full time job right now. I may have a PhD in it shortly.

November 30

Glass balls and rubber balls. Glass balls are things in life that need to be cared for and attended to. They are the most important. Rubber balls are the things in life that can be dropped and not break. They are things in life that are not quite as precious as our glass balls. When juggling all of the responsibilities of life, it's so important to stop and see which are which, and to make sure we're not dropping the glass balls because our hands are full with the rubber ones. It can be easy to confuse the rubber for glass based on societal pressures or paradigms. It can all seem so overwhelming— like it's impossible to carry and juggle all of the balls when we are confused and think that they are all glass. My glass balls are the emotional and physical wellbeing of the people who are most important to me. I am included on that list. Death and grief teach you just how fragile those glass balls can be. It shows you that there are actually very few glass balls, and they are all relationships of importance. Relationships and love trump social commitments, career, status, reputation, material things, etc. I found the clarity of what is actually important when we moved on to the boat after losing my uncle and my dad. I regret forgetting again and not using my grief and love for long-term enlightenment. I regret falling into the societal trap again, but I see so clearly now. I am grateful for that deep felt clarity to guide the rest of my life. And I am dedicated to being conscious and keeping this enlightenment for the rest of my life.

December 1

I can get caught up in the worry of what we have no control over, like worrying about my loved ones and how they are faring after this loss. Worry about money or any myriad of things. I was talking with a fellow bereaved mom, and we were acknowledging that our worry seems so silly after we have already experienced the worst possible thing, and even after that worst possible thing, we know without a shadow of a doubt that our babies are whole, beautiful, thriving and ever present. So, why are we worrying?! We know that from a soul perspective, it's all more than okay. My boyfriend owns a care home. I've gotten to know the residents over time, and we know that one of them is actively dying. Her transition will be soon. The old me would have felt sad and maybe a little bit scared of the whole process. Today, I felt excited and happy for her. She gets to go home and close this amazing chapter of growth. Connect with kindred souls. Be out of her heavy and malfunctioning body. What a sacred time! Just as the birth of a new soul on Earth in the form of a baby is sacred, to be birthed into a different dimension upon your human body's death is just the other side of this special and sacred coin! If we can stay in our knowing of this transition and that our energy and consciousness never dies, death loses its hold over how we live. We no longer have to stay in emotional suffering. We no longer have to worry. We no longer have to fear physical death. It opens us up to living life based on our alignment and betterment of mankind and not making choices out of fear.

December 2

I had a weekend filled with relaxation and mindfulness. Reading and getting into my spiritual/higher self mindset. I felt as close to myself as I have in the past several months. I felt like I was onto something. I was hopeful. I find that when I'm zoned out without something to focus on, it triggers my flashbacks and moments of panic. We went for a long, mindless walk and I was overcome with panic at the thought that in my "real" life, Noah is dead. I was frantic to get back to my higher self, knowing that Noah is not gone. Knowing that this is just Earth life and we are so much more than this moment in time. I read something today that said this coming back to knowing our higher self/soul is a reset switch. It's our safety valve when everything feels like too much. We can't always stay in this higher self state of mind as humans. But with focus and intention, we can stay there longer and catch ourselves when we've fallen back into the trap of thinking we are only human and this life on Earth is all there is. I've realized that emptying my mind is not the goal. It's to slow it down enough to focus on love or gratitude. To feel it in my body. This leaves no room for panic, flashbacks, or despair. This is a constant spiral into my humanness with the insight from my stillness. Into my stillness from moments of human fear or hopelessness. I believe that as the spiral evolves, there is more hope and less despair. Having a safety valve where we shift our perspective higher, outside of our limited human minds to observe ourselves in our role on Earth is essential to not only getting through life, but to engage with life in a growth oriented and meaningful way.

December 3

Did you know that venting has actually been shown to make mental and emotional health worse?[5] I knew in my gut that there was no amount of talk therapy that would help me. In fact the therapy I've engaged in that was focused on talking made me feel worse. I've had friends from out of state call regularly to check in. I find myself avoiding these calls because I anticipate the question: How have you been doing? And if I respond to that, it means I have to rehash what I have felt in the past. I value and appreciate talking about how I'm feeling in the present moment so I can try to make sense of it, acknowledge it, and use it to help me in my healing process. But I have that visceral feeling of not wanting to vent or rehash. And now I'm realizing it's because it makes me feel worse. It ingrains the sad story in my head. I relive the traumatic moments that I've experienced since Noah's transition. I would likely include my ahas and triumphs, but they are in relation to the intense trials, and I don't want to feel all of it over again. It becomes my narrative. When the reality is that my narrative is ever evolving. It changes day by day, hour by hour. I am making sense of how my body, brain, and soul are responding to this sudden loss. But repeating the process that is now in the past is painful and unproductive. I know I need to feel (although I don't always want to; sometimes it feels too scary), attempt to understand, and do what it takes to progress in my healing.

---

5. Sophie L. Kjaervik and Brad J. Bushman, "A meta-analytic review of anger management activities that increase or decrease arousal: What fuels or douses rage?" *Science Direct* 109 (2024), https://doi.org/10.1016/j.cpr.2024.102414.

December 4

This boy was so protective and sweet with his little sister. It melts my heart to look back and see it with fresh eyes—in every picture he is holding her or helping her. Death needs

a rebrand. Instead of using the word death, can we call it Rebirth? A Rebirth into another chapter of existence and growth. A Rebirth into the newest most expanded version of us that has yet to exist? Can we shift the current paradigm that so many of us inherit from our families and society of our human body's death being an awful thing, to it being like a butterfly going through its metamorphosis? To it being a part of the infinite spiral of life, growth, and rebirth. When we have a Celebration of Life, can we actually mean it? Celebrate with a deep knowing that their Rebirth was a big milestone in their journey, just as their initial birth onto Earth was? Celebrate our capacity to evolve and connect with spirit? Celebrate the great gift to those left on Earth given by Rebirth to reconnect with their purpose in life, their capacity for love, and their remembrance that life is so much more than our daily tasks. That we are so much more than we give ourselves credit for. Can we acknowledge that our human brains will struggle to comprehend and accept the physical absence of someone who is so special, present, and important? That we know the heartache and grief that comes with a physical loss is part of the brain's natural response?

That we have the power to shift our paradigm whenever we want to create our own realities? That if we truly listen to the heart and not just the brain, we know that our special soul did not die and that we are always connected?

December 5

Noah ended his human life two weeks after receiving a diagnosis of persistent depressive disorder, which he was told is resistant to treatment and would likely be something he would need help managing for the rest of his life. Did you know that the risk of suicide attempts is significantly increased within ninety days after a mental health diagnosis?[6] Do you know why we have "diagnoses"? The DSM (the manual used to diagnose mental health disorders) was created for insurance companies, so they could bill and decide if someone actually needed services/treatment.[7] It is now used for medication as well. What is included in this manual changes over time because as a society we realize that some things we pathologize are just part of being human. I would argue that many, if not most, diagnoses fall in this category. Apparently it's not enough for someone to present with symptoms and say that they need help. Symptoms of loneliness, apathy, hopelessness, despair. They have to be labeled with a diagnosis. The very act of diagnosing and being labeled by a doctor or mental health professional as having a condition that is lifelong or difficult to treat feels like a death sentence. And increases the risk of suicide. There is no actual need to define this for someone. How do we know what their life will be like? Can we offer support without giving someone a label that indicates even more hopelessness? The system needs to change. A reliance on diagnosis for access to help is insane. We have gotten so far away from connecting human to human. We

---

6. Jason R. Randall et al, "Acute Risk of Suicide and Suicide Attempts Associated With Recent Diagnosis of Mental Disorders: A Population-Based, Propensity Score–Matched Analysis," *The Canadian Journal of Psychiatry* 59, no. 10 (2014), doi:10.1177/070674371405901006.

7. Sally Satel, "Why the Fuss Over the D.S.M.-5?" quoted in "DSM matters for insurance, services, but little else," National Education Alliance for Borderline Personality Disorder, posted May 11, 2013, https://www.borderlinepersonalitydisorder.org/dsm-matters-for-insurance-services-but-little-else/.

have become so sterile and "by the book." Labels increase stigma, isolation, and hopelessness. Prevention, normalization, connection. We need more of this.

December 6

In 2023, Noah and I went on an epic trip to Thailand. I decided I wanted to do one-on-one trips with the kids because they all have different interests and like doing different things. I rarely got to spend individual time with them. I can't tell you how grateful I am for this time with him. I didn't just love Noah because he was my son. I truly felt a deep connection with him. He got me. And I thought I got him. I really enjoyed his company. His humor. Wit. Intelligence. His adventurous and laid back nature. I was really looking forward to being more of his friend in addition to his mom as he got older. My purpose in continuing to share my experiences with Noah before and after he transitioned is twofold. First, to help those move through their grief when that time arises (because it will). Life never stays the same and life-changing grief comes in many forms. Secondly, to help people think about what life means and become inspired to live their purpose with love. To get real. I will continue to do this work and share it through retreats, speaking, workshops, and books. I also want to educate folks. To advocate. On depression, suicide, systemic issues, and to grow a group of like-minded people who want to make a real change in the world. If you feel inspired to share my words with others you think it might resonate with, I encourage you to do so. I love you.

December 7

During Covid, our dog Charlie passed away. Several months later, Noah begged us for a dog. My husband, at the time, and I were going through a separation, and I didn't think it would be a good idea to get a dog with all of the transition happening. But I could tell how important it was to him, so we eventually caved and adopted a dog named Marley. Noah renamed her Mia. We decided she was the kids' dog, so she travels between my house and their dad's house. She was feral when we got her—wouldn't let anyone touch her, she wouldn't come inside, etc. It was awful. But after a few months of earning her trust, she came inside, let us touch her, and now won't leave our sides. She has been our therapy dog. A true angel for our family during the divorce, teen years, and now the loss of Noah's physical presence. As I reflect, I think she is the glue that has held us together. She is the sweetest, most loving, gentle, and calming baby I've ever encountered. To say we are attached to her is an understatement. I've often thought since Noah transitioned that Mia can't leave us. That I don't know what I would do if the kids had to experience that loss. But the reality is, that it will happen someday. And we need to reckon with our attachment to her. Soaking her up every second we have her. Just as with any valued relationship in our lives. She didn't seem well yesterday, and as I monitored her through the night, I couldn't keep my mind from thinking about how we just couldn't handle another loss. How I thought I had worked through the ideas of attachment and suffering, but I found myself begging Noah and spirit to make sure she's okay. I thought about how I'm stuck in this feeling of attachment and fear of loss, and how letting go of attachment is critical. It made me think about the difference between love and attachment. We do easily become attached to those we love. And grief rears its ugly head when we love and are attached at the same time, but also when we love and aren't attached. We can't escape grief. But we can lessen the suffering that comes along with it when we embrace acceptance and non-attachment. This thought process begs the question: What exactly is grief? I think grief is a combination of our human brains feeling as if we have lost our connection, our loss of future memories we were attached to having, and the sorrow of knowing our loved one won't have any of the future memories that they were attached to.

And what is the difference between connection and attachment? We all want to feel connected. And we all ARE connected—there is no denying that. But I think often, when we lose someone, we think that if we don't feel the sorrow that comes with attachment that we didn't really love them. But I wonder if that is just the paradigm we have created for ourselves. What if because we loved them, we release them from attachment?

This bouncing from thought to thought is my new existence. Welcome to the non-stop movement of my brain in grief.

December 8

A very real and vulnerable share … I used to be bubbly, bold, energetic, funny, engaging, confident, enthusiastic, and social. Last night I tried another holiday party. I was doing pretty well for the first half. I noticed my nervous system was starting to overload and then the dreaded question came up after I had talked about Grant and Hope: So you have two children? I fumbled my words, and my host was caught off guard. Within seconds the conversation shifted back to the house remodel. My son died, and I went from saying that out loud to talking about a house remodel. I had been in a good place about feeling Noah around me and trying to be positive about his rebirth into the spiritual realm—not death. But the normal reaction to hearing about the death of a child is sympathy, shock, and sorrow. I don't know how to stay in this space of knowing and feeling my connection with him and feeling others' reflection back to me of the pain they imagine I am feeling. I was a bit shaken up and while trying to multitask, texting Grant and going down stairs, I tripped and dislocated my finger. My finger looked like the number 7, a complete 90-degree angle, and I became light headed and nearly passed out. I made a scene and was quite embarrassed. I've said a few times since Noah passed that I don't belong in public. I feel like people see me as this sad version of who I used to be. Instead of confident, I feel scared of how my nervous system will react in a situation. Instead of engaging, I want to be a wallflower so no one asks about my children. I know I have value and I want to be seen for more than who I am currently presenting as. I don't know how to engage in the world. Writing is a safe place where I can try to connect without the risk of imploding in public. Being around others who have experienced loss or are vulnerable is another safe space. As much as I preach and believe in the importance of community and vulnerability, I struggle with feeling as if I am being a downer or ruining a good time. I think I can only continue to try to figure out my place in the world, showing up some days feeling inspired and inspiring, and some days wearing my human pain visibly.

December 9

Noah and I are headed on a little impromptu adventure. I bought a ticket on Friday, after learning that I could join my friend on a work trip in Milan this week. I'm very much looking forward to the anonymity and language barrier. Somewhere I can be without engaging with anyone who will ask me anything I don't want to talk about. To step out of my day-to-day survival mode. I know we can't run away from our feelings or realities, but travel always allows for such an easy shift in perspective. And connecting with friends who don't live nearby is therapy in and of itself. I like knowing I can take Noah with me anywhere I want to go. A constant travel companion. I was texting a friend info on the hotel I was going to stay at, and Noah's airdrop popped up on my phone. His phone line is still active. I haven't been able to bring myself to deactivate it. It sits on the kitchen counter, plugged in, but never opened. I think this was him telling me he's headed there with me. Today, I am feeling overwhelmed with love for my amazing children. Gratitude for their beautiful souls that I have been gifted with ushering into this iteration of their Earthly life. Knowing that while we are parent and child in this reality, we are connected in such a bigger way. I don't see Noah as my baby in his current form. I see him as a powerful, loving soul that is teaching and guiding me. And if we can open our hearts to see it now, we can move through life knowing we are each other's teachers even in these roles we are currently playing in each other's lives on Earth. My soul family. With no hierarchy. Just love. And Gratitude. I love you.

Month
6

December 10

On my first adventure out of the hotel room today in Milan, I stumbled upon a Christmas market near the Duomo Piazza. I was browsing and then looked up to find countless Purple Hearts in front of me. I proceeded to cry loving tears as I walked around this absolutely stunning town, knowing that Noah was tagging right along. I saw men selling red roses and I thought to myself that if I somehow ended up with one, it was Noah's doing. Lo and behold, while eating at an outdoor cafe, a man tried to sell one to me. I kept saying, "No, grazie," but he was insistent, so we went round and round for a minute. The kind gentleman next to me must have felt the awkwardness and pulled out ten euros, and the rose salesman gave me three roses. I thanked him and got teary eyed because I know Noah made that happen. So, today's update is, I'm walking around Milan crying and grateful. I love you.

December 11

My room last night had a direct view of the Virgin Mary—I could see her soaring high above the city. It felt comforting to see her, as I had just been reminded that Mary was also a bereaved mother. As I walked through the duomo I noticed many statues and paintings of mother and child. And many depicting life and death. Joy and torture. Human existence. I was reminded that I am not the only mother experiencing this pain. And that life and death are central themes of our existence. It somehow feels comforting to know that I am being held by those that have come before me. That I am not blazing this path on my own. I lit a candle in the church for Noah and took a moment to appreciate all of the unknown. The mystery. The mind boggling nature of our existence. And to feel the depth of my love for him as my heart bursts with emotion. Right now equal parts inexplicable love and indescribable pain. And maybe, hopefully someday, mostly love.

December 12

A couple of days after Noah transitioned, a mom friend who is very spiritually connected, told me that Noah had come to her and showed her a heart with a line through it to signify that he would not let us fall too far. That when it felt like we couldn't take anymore heartache, he would put someone in our path to help us or let us know without a doubt that he continues to exist, happily, and is with us. She even went so far as to paint the heart  with the line that she saw. Maybe a week later Hope looked up in the sky and captured this. She sent it via text and I reminded her that this was Noah's sign to us. This is one of my favorite pictures and signs from Noah. I have felt him very close, and I have, on many occasions, told him that it's too much, I need his help. And somehow something will implant in my mind that provides comfort or a new and helpful connection appears. Noah has shown himself to be dependable, loving, powerful, present, and devoted. Just as he was in human form. That is his essence. I love you.

December 13

Today I had a little spa day. One of the things about grief is that your entire body hurts. It's like you have a constant flu. You ache and are tense everywhere. And funny enough, even though I'm a massage therapist, I haven't had a massage locally while grieving because I've been scared. It seems impossible to find trauma-informed and grief-educated practitioners. To me, this is a huge gap in the market. I have never needed massage therapy more, and I can't find someone to trust to deliver it. To know how to handle a flashback or panic attack. To know how to lessen the chance of those things happening. To hold space for my tears. Today, I thought I was in a headspace where I could do it. And then, right before I arrived I started to feel the anxiety creep in. While I love the use of massage to enter a meditative state, that calm mind can be a blank canvas for those who suffer from flashbacks. That happened today and my eyes shot open, heart racing. And I worked on finding my resource image, focusing on the touch sensations I was feeling, and implementing vagal breathing to avoid a panic attack. When they guided me into the resting room afterwards, I broke down. Luckily it was just me. And then the lamp directly across from me turned off and then on all by itself. I thanked Noah for showing me his presence. But, God, what I would give to see him again. Laugh with him again. Hear him tease me, which then made me reminisce out loud to Noah about our fancy spa date in Bangkok where I booked a couples massage because I thought he'd be more comfortable with me there. They had us get into a couples tub to soak beforehand and we sat awkwardly shoulder to shoulder laughing about our weird mother-son massage experience. These are the days. Thinking I'm functioning well, thinking about how I can make the world a better place from and through my experiences, and then crumbling. And the cycle continues. I think it's a spiral instead of a never ending circle, making small progress along the way.

December 14

The one stand out takeaway from my trip to Milan is how friendly everyone has been. Not in a rush. Happy to engage in conversation. It has not been lost on me how important it is to connect with others in our daily interactions. I've learned about Milanese culture, and even with the language barrier, I seemed to connect through smiles, extra limoncello offered, hugs, and shoulder pats. All levels of connection are important. The short, seemingly inconsequential daily interactions, the relationships that last only a few months, the long term relationships ... they are all important because they all remind us that we are connected. That we are not alone. And that we all share a similar experience.

December 15

"They" say it takes time to learn how to live in this new reality. That time is the greatest tool that can ease the suffering of losing someone. I think it is more than just time—it has to be about the specific, sometimes intentional, and sometimes organic experiences that come with time. The experience of feeling the spirit connection. The experience of learning how to continue to express your love beyond our physical form. The experience of witnessing others who are making their way. The experience of learning to talk about them and to them everyday. The experience of feeling the intensity of emotion and knowing that it's possible to surface from the depths over and over again. The experience of having everything you thought you knew stripped away and learning what your new foundation/truth is. The experience of owning and acting on that truth. We can actually work with our grief, actively experiencing things to process and invite in growth. Alternatively, with the passage of time, no active engagement with our grief, we instead bury it away and have it feel less intense in our bodies and hearts over time. But if we dig enough, it will still be there. Heavy and impacting our lives in ways we can't see. Let's be real and actively engaged instead of just letting time pass as a means of "healing." I love you.

December 16

As part of my mission to prevent depression from taking hold by getting to the root cause of depression, and offering real, effective options beyond the medication and individual therapy status quo, I feel called to help those grieving to learn how to digest it skillfully. In a way that transmutes the sorrow to something beautiful. For me, this work IS how I am transmuting my grief. I know the depths of sorrow and I have a unique perspective that incorporates both my professional background and personal, lived experiences. I feel deep in my heart that I am supposed to take this experience and help change the conversation and work around grief, life and death. Did you know that parents who lose a child are significantly more likely to die by health issues and suicide in the three years following the child's death than parents who have not lost a child?[8] And that poor mental health outcomes persist, no matter how long the child has been gone? And that the one thing that has been associated with improved mental and physical health is by finding purpose and meaning in life? This work is so important. It is literally life or death for those in deep grief. And we need more than talk therapy. We need to dive deep into existential work to figure out what our purpose is for being alive when our child isn't. This work will be for bereaved parents, of course. But also for anyone that is feeling the call to lift their own depression by diving deep. Anyone who has experienced a profound loss and is struggling. I love you.

---

8. Jieun Song, Marsha R. Mailick, Jan S. Greenberg, and Frank J. Floyd, "Mortality in parents after the death of a child," *Social Sciences & Medicine* 239 (2019), https://doi.org/10.1016/j.socscimed.2019.112522.

December 17

I just heard someone make an analogy of not being able to prove that love exists and not knowing if a soul connection after physical death exists. There is no way to "prove" love. You just have a knowing that it exists, that you feel it for someone and from someone. It's just a feeling. A trust in the concept of love. The same can be said for knowing that a soul's love and connection never dies. But some kind of "proof" helps. Love with someone on Earth in human form is demonstrated through commitment, honesty, time, and affection. For an infinite soul connection, it's more abstract and sometimes even very direct signs. But for some who have more doubt or their brains create barriers to seeing the signs, even more impactful is a reading from a medium. I've realized that the work of trusted and evidence-based mediums (yes, that's a thing) is critically important for many who are grieving. We have our internal knowing, but the external "proof" means so much. I have wondered how many lives the work of evidence-based mediums have saved. The peace that comes from confirmation that your loved one is with you and doing well is the most beautiful gift one can receive and the one thing that can keep you going as a bereaved parent. If you are looking for an evidence-based medium, you can find them on the Helping Parents Heal website.

December 18

Today I noticed that I was feeling sorry for myself. Some days I have a little pity party. I told my therapist that I hated to admit it, but I was feeling sorry for myself. Her response was surprising. She said, "Good, you should." And wow, I needed to hear that. I've been working so hard on processing, figuring out how to make meaning, how to survive each day, how to forgive myself, how to help others, how to be the best mom I can to Hope and Grant as we all navigate this trauma together, how to deal with the logistics of life and work in this new reality, etc.—that I've successfully avoided fully acknowledging the horror that I've experienced. I don't think I've been ready, because fully acknowledging it feels like it might actually kill me, nearly six months after. My body and brain couldn't handle it any sooner. I suppose this is the next phase. Fully honoring the depth of loss and its impact on me as a regular human being who doesn't possess super strength. Who needs to be cared for. Who needs others. Who needs a soft place to land within myself and with others. I can't do this alone. No one can. I've forgotten to give much time or attention to acknowledging the thread of grief that has been woven throughout my life. To feel compassion and grace for this woman who has experienced many heartaches in life, including the greatest heartache one could imagine. If you are struggling with Noah's loss, please reach out to me. I love you.

December 19

Tonight on our way to Hope's band performance, we were reminiscing about Noah making funny faces at Grant when he was the one performing, trying to make him laugh. Noah always made him laugh. That was one of my favorite things to witness. Those two good naturedly teasing each other. These memories make me smile and feel a pang in my gut at the same time. He was so good. And funny. And sweet. And considerate. And I miss him. It was and is sweet to witness the kids desire to be there for each other at their performances, birthdays, promotions, etc. They genuinely want to be there for each other. We feel the huge hole when Noah is missing from that equation. And at the same time, I feel so grateful for all three of my sweet, loving, and thoughtful kids. I try to maintain the mindset that he is even more present and supportive in spirit form, which I do actually believe. But I wonder when the lump in my throat and the pit in my stomach will go away when I think about never experiencing Noah physically again, in this lifetime. A dear friend reminded me that my connection will deepen even more once I've reached acceptance. I'm on the road, because I know that is the only way to continue to live, but I know I have not quite reached it. I love you sweet boy. So much. I feel you and think of you in every moment.

December 20

I remember the first time I put on clothes, waterproof mascara, lipstick, and blow dried my hair after Noah passed. It felt incongruent with how I felt on the inside, and I felt self conscious looking like I had it together on the outside when my son had just died a month earlier. And I received comments on it from my therapist and friends. It made me feel that in order to be seen for how I really feel, I should look like shit. But if I was going to get out of bed and do the work that had to be done to care for Grant and Hope, I had to get up in the morning, shower, get dressed, and ready. My days are better when I have a reason to get up and ready. Going to therapy is sometimes the only thing I do in a day when I don't have Grant and Hope, and I use that as an excuse to get up and ready.

I am all too familiar with how easy it is to get sucked into depression and have to fight to get moving again. An object in motion stays in motion. And I must stay in motion for Grant and Hope.

Some days I encounter a sales clerk or receptionist, looking normal. And I think to myself, you have no idea that I just lost my son. That I am dying inside. And that it took everything I had to get up and ready to go grocery shopping or to the doctor. I smile and greet them. Knowing my world has just been turned upside down and they have no idea.

It's so important to treat everyone with grace and kindness. You never know what is happening internally. Never judge a book by its cover. The kindness of strangers has a much bigger impact than you know. Each day when I can leave the house and I have encountered kindness I notice, and I am beyond grateful.

December 21

I keep coming back to the idea that we grieve everything and everyone that isn't in the exact present moment. Grant found a video of the four-year-old version of himself the other day. It was the cutest damn thing I've seen in a long while and my heart was breaking and bursting at the exact same time. Tears of missing him at this age and loving him now flowed simultaneously. How will I never get to experience the sweetness of four-year-old Grant again? And how grateful am I to have experienced him at all?

I have heard more than one person lately say how surprised they are at how well I seem to be doing. I know I technically have an option, but in my mind I don't. How could I ever give up time with Grant and Hope in the precious moments I still have with them? If this has taught me nothing else, it's to revel in every moment we have with our loves.

And that is where I am training my mind to go when I feel the heartbreak of losing Noah ... to go to how grateful I am for our time together.

When I feel myself spiraling, I recite the Ho'oponopono[9] prayer over and over:

I'm sorry. Please forgive me. Thank you. I love you.

But with a focus on the, "Thank you" and "I love you."

We've all heard that all we have is the present, and I think we often nod our heads and know on a surface level that this is true. But, I am feeling this in my core, and it's bringing up new grief about losing yesterday, while also bringing up a new depth of gratitude for today and yesterday.

Love your people today. And that includes you. I love you.

---

9. Created in 1976 by Morrnah Nalamaku Simeona, daughter of one of the last Hawaiian priestesses, as a prayer for correction and balance.

December 22

Hope and I made paintings for Noah's Christmas gift today. I don't consider myself artistic, so I've been surprised at the role art has played in my processing. I've painted my visions related to my PTSD, depictions of my dreams and meditations with Noah, and also how I see us still connected. It helps me sort what's in my head and gives me a comforting image to look to when I need it. And it gives me a way to consciously connect with him.

December 23

Self-compassion is limited without the perspective that we are souls in a human body with a human brain. I've found that self-compassion is a big part of healing from Noah ending his life. And I could not comprehend self-compassion until I was able to zoom out and see this life for what it is. I'm reflecting on many of the self-help principles: staying in the present moment, gratitude, cognitive-behavioral work to put our problems in perspective, mind-body regulation, etc. They all make so much more sense to me when I add in the soul component. When I think about life in the context of Soul Work, I'm able to shift and have more compassion for my human self. Earth work is hard! I can visualize my soul wrapping my human form in love and grace—with a deep knowing that I am whole and full of love and light at my core. I'm experiencing struggle for a reason. My efforts to grow are applauded and my missteps are not judged. This translates to how I can show up for and have compassion for others as well. Seeing us all as these beautiful souls trying our best in Earth school. We are all the same. So much compassion and love for my sweet Noah and everyone struggling in our human form. I love you.

December 24

Presence. I've had a hard time with this. Many times when I am having a conversation, I have the reminder that Noah has transitioned running in the back of my head. I'm not present. Sometimes I'm present for a few minutes, and then I remind myself of my reality and feel like a horrible mom that I forgot for a few minutes that my son took his life. I had a realization last night. I had the story running in the back of my head about Noah being gone as my boyfriend was talking. I thought to myself I could pretend and smile along, or I could be real and tell him I was having trouble being present and let him know what I was thinking. Just the simple act of being real brought me into the present moment. And I realized during our conversation that just because I'm being present with someone doesn't mean I don't care about all of the other people I'm not with in that moment. That the people who are important to me get my dedicated and devoted time and attention. That includes Noah. Everyday. I can carve out dedicated time to be with Noah just as I can with my Earth-side loves. So, maybe I can give myself permission to be present for all of the other people in my life and not feel guilty about it. That it's actually a reflection of my love for him and them if I can be fully present for all of the people in my life. Because when we aren't fully present, we are not actually connecting or engaging in an authentic way. Our soul isn't a part of the equation; instead, it's just an empty head nod, smile, and a half-listening brain. No heart. I want heart connections. I want everyone to feel my love fully. Those Earth-side and those in spirit form.

December 25

I have not been able to go through and send thank yous for all of the cards, flowers, meals, books, etc. that people have sent us just yet. But I want to take this opportunity to give my heartfelt thank you and gratitude for all of the love our family has received. Life is about love and connection. Thank you for loving Noah. Thank you for showing your care for us. I'm looking forward to the time when we have our feet under us enough to give back in a big way. In the meantime, I love you.

December 26

Noah showed up for us big time for Christmas. He's such a powerful soul, working so hard to show us he's with us. Thank you, Noah. We love you.

December 27

Bravery. Common refrains heard after the loss of a loved one include, "You are so strong," "I don't know how you're doing it—I could never," "You have to stay strong for the kids and put on a brave face." I used to think that being strong was being stoic, containing emotion, engaging in normal life as soon as possible, etc. Now I see that as a protective mechanism so you don't have to fully face the loss. A form of denial of the gravity of loss you've experienced. Now, I see that bravery is facing the depth of emotion that is present in the body. To feel the assault felt to the soul. To be real and to share that depth of emotion with others and not hide it. To honor taking baby steps and honoring what is needed to care for a broken heart instead of hiding, stuffing, and returning to normal day-to-day activities. It's scary to fully feel. It feels overwhelming and sometimes like it will actually kill you. It doesn't have to be all at once. Baby steps are okay. I see the bravery and value in slowly feeling and processing it all. The gift of grief is wasted if we don't transmute it and use it to grow.

December 28

"Against the natural order." "This wasn't supposed to happen." "What a tragedy." All common refrains about physical death. These refrains make it hard for me to engage in normal society where others view Noah's transition this way. Death happens every day. It happens in every life. Suicide happens every day. The death of a child happens every day. Deaths from causes that aren't "natural" happen every day. As part of a community of bereaved mothers, I see that I am part of a large group of people. I'm not unique. I am living life. I will experience death. Maybe sooner than some. But with life comes death. With life comes sorrow. With life comes love. For every human. Physical death is not an accident or mistake. Proof of consciousness after our bodies die exists. We have created a paradigm that causes suffering. That death is tragic. There is a reason for death. It is a portal to eternal life. A portal for those still in human bodies to remember why we are here. We aren't meant to live forever. Death isn't the death we've made it out to be. It's a returning of physical matter to the Earth. And a transportation of our souls and consciousness to a different dimension. When you lose someone you are required to look deeper. I invite you to look deeper with me.

December 29

Detachment and devotion: These two words have been front and center for me since Noah's transition. Both are critical. If I stay attached to the idea that Noah should be alive in his physical form then I create suffering for myself. I think when we find ourselves using the word "should" in any capacity, we are headed down the road of attachment and suffering. Noah shouldn't be here in physical form at this moment in time, or he would be. His transition has had a ripple effect in our community. It will shape how people move forward in their lives. It offers the opportunity to devote our lives to living from a place of love, connection, acceptance—to make the world a better place. And his ability to help us and guide us from his spirit form, if we let him, is a blessing. If I can detach from this idea, then I make room for devotion to my love for him. I can use my energy to focus on love and gratitude for his role in my life—past, present, and future. I leave room for devotion to living a life filled with gratitude and love ... in my relationships, in my work, and for myself. This is daily work. And I'm not always successful at staying in this place of detachment and devotion, at being at peace with the present, and at the same time, be filled with love and devotion for him. It's work that takes dedication and devotion. But I can think of no better way to spend my life than to live a life dedicated to love as a testament to my immense love for my son.

December 30

Embodiment versus dissociation: The wellness world talks about the importance of embodiment with a focus on always feeling fully in your body or connecting the mind and the body. The mental health world pathologizes dissociation (or not being in the body) as bad and something needs to be fixed. I have a different perspective. I think both embodiment and dissociation are critically important to accessing both your higher self and coming back to the groundedness that allows us to live our human lives without going crazy. We can't stay in full embodiment or full dissociation and be our full human/spirit selves. We need to identify and embrace both. Dissociation can be protective if the brain and body aren't ready to fully feel something. It can be a tool to access the soul and realize we are not our brains or bodies, but a greater consciousness. It's a dance we must make between moments of full embodiment and stepping out of our bodies to access our full consciousness and soul wisdom. We must consciously move between both worlds. Honoring your body when it doesn't feel emotionally safe to be fully in your body. And taking the wisdom we receive from dissociating from our brains and bodies to know we are a soul in a human body. We are more than what we think with our human brains. The work as I see it is to figure out how to skillfully move between both worlds, knowing when we need to be embodied or when we need to access our higher selves.

December 31

I have been fascinated with learning about near death experiences—what happens right after we physically die. One of the common experiences among people who have died and come back to life is the "life review." In this review you see every little interaction you've had with others in life and not only see, but feel what the other person, animal, etc. felt as a result and how that interaction influenced their interactions. Upon return to their body on Earth, there is a knowing that we are all connected. That our interactions have a ripple effect that extends far beyond what we think. This knowing also occurs for many after taking psychedelics. If we are all connected, then we understand that what we do to or for someone else impacts us. Selflessness is selfish. It goes beyond the golden rule to treat others as you would like to be treated. Instead, how we treat others is how we are treating ourselves because we are all one—there is no "other." This is exciting and terrifying—the ripple is huge—good or bad. We have so much power in just our daily interactions. My intention for the New Year is to engage in life with that life review in mind. Thinking about how my words and actions impact the souls around me. This is Soul Work and conscious living. And just maybe, is the reason we are here. I love you. May your year be filled with love, connection and growth.

January 1

Thank you to those of you who have shared how Noah's story and that of our family's healing journey has impacted you. That is the ripple effect I spoke of in my last post. The seemingly small things that make a big difference. Many days I don't know what I'm doing. I'm just sharing as a dedication to Noah's life and our suffering/love for him. Often I don't even realize what I've written until I'm done and take a moment to read it before posting. When this happens I feel like it's Noah speaking through me, and his messages are important for my processing and healing. I hope to help others in their own grief journeys as well. Small notes of encouragement or awareness—to know that you are listening—means more than you know. I love you.

January 2

Somehow today feels just like the day he left us. I went for an appointment to help my brain move through this trauma, and lo and behold it was in an office three doors down from Noah's therapist's office. Where he was two days before he chose to end his physical life. As I punched in the door code and went up the elevator, I wondered what had been going through his head and heart the last time he was there. It took me back. The grief is all encompassing—body, mind, and soul. Today, I am sick and I'm realizing how much a high-functioning, well taken care of physical body impacts the whole. I love you, Noah. I'm trying so hard. Today feels intense. Being embodied is too painful today. I'm taking the day off from trying to be fully human.

January 3

No words today. Just love.

January 4

*"What are you afraid of losing, when nothing in the
world actually belongs to you?" —Marcus Aurelius*

I've been struggling ... and just after a grief fit, I saw this quote on
a Facebook account titled "Days of Noah." It caught my attention
because of the account name. It felt like a message from Noah.
I'm suffering because I feel as though I have been stripped of
something. Of a relationship. Of a future. Of the life I wanted for
Noah, his siblings, and myself. One that included him, a happy and
engaged-in-life version of him. But, I am once again reminded that
Noah did not belong to me. He was his own human. On his own
journey. We are guaranteed nothing. No one belongs to us or owes
us anything. Our time and experiences with one another are a gift.

January 5

It can feel heavy being a soul in these bodies. Bodies that get sick, hurt, tired, old. It's obvious that the body, mind, and soul all have to work together to make the most out of this human experience. The state of one impacts the others. I've been the sickest I can remember the past few days and am finally coming out on the other side of it today. The pain in my body made my mind weak, and my weak mind hurt my soul. I felt like I had nothing to give and nothing mattered. I feel like I've been able to figure out how to manage my mind's impact on my body and soul. I know what resources to seek out and implement that help me. And through my spiritual studies and work, I understand and have agency over my soul's impact on my mind and body. But this made me realize I am highly susceptible to my body negatively impacting my mind and soul. I thought about what we can learn from those who live life with physical disability, or chronic illness and pain. It seems all-consuming when you are in it. I imagine this is how Noah felt in both his body and mind. He hadn't found ways to alleviate the pain, so it wasn't all consuming. What a hard place to be—to feel as if you are dying and not knowing a solution to alleviate the pain. No amount of love can take that pain away. Being a human is hard with our challenging minds and heavy, sometimes painful bodies and brains. When there is no respite or hope for a better future, and our present is highly painful, how do we go on? I think it has to be related to understanding your own purpose in life. There has to be an existential inquiry. A conversation with your soul. We need to be reminded of that before we're suffering and come back to that foundation when we're suffering. We have to consciously live to know how to withstand the eventual hardships that life will deal us. Start having those conversations with your kiddos early. I wish I had.

January 6

What do I mean by connection? I've talked a lot about the importance of connection and the impact of loneliness on mental and emotional health. It's important to recognize that you can feel the loneliest you've ever felt in the company of others if you don't feel seen, heard, validated, and have commonalities at a deep level. Sometimes I think when we worry about others, it puts our mind at ease to know they aren't "alone." When we see them out and about or being social, it allows us to write them off as doing well. But being social or having people around you and feeling truly connected don't always co-exist. It takes time and intentional vulnerability to create such relationships. Building true connection is so important.

January 7

On every beach I set foot on, for the rest of my life. NOAH

January 8

Today I sat down to contemplate and write down what my intentions are for the new year. I sat in the same seat, at the same hotel, in the same coastal town as I did last year. I opened my journal to find what I had written last year and emotion overtook me. I had so many specific visions for my year ahead. Visions that assumed I didn't experience a great trauma. That assumed my family was healthy, happy, and whole. Not very many of my "goals" came to fruition this past year and it all seemed pretty trivial now, looking back. I can see from both sides now, the desire to be in a place where the trivial goals seemed important. To have that carefree and light perspective. But I also see the other side now— the immense growth that has taken place on its own—without it being written as part of my plan for myself and my family.

This year, my intentions are much more broad and acknowledge that life has its own path in store for me. The intentions I want to bring to the forefront of my being everyday are to be present. To love. And to be open.

I believe that keeping presence, love, and openness can help me survive when I am in the most challenging season of my life, and also to thrive when I'm in a "coasting" period (looking forward to when that happens!).

January 9

While I do see the importance of presence, it's still a hard one for me. Because in my current present moment, Noah is not alive in his body, not accessible to me. So, how can staying in the present moment give me peace? I think I have to take it a step further by being present while also knowing that nothing is promised or guaranteed in each moment. If I live in the past, I will suffer because I long for memories or wish I could have changed an outcome. If I live in the future, I worry or again long for a future that is no longer possible. If I stay in the present, I sit with reality. I can embrace what I have been given in this moment in time. The presence of a friend. A good meal. A walk on the beach. My dedicated time to talk to and feel Noah in his spirit form. A snuggle with my Earth-side kiddos, etc. Noticing the space between thoughts. Witnessing your thoughts as separate from your soul. Presence is not about having everything you want in this moment, but focusing on gratitude for what you do have and are experiencing. Presence is fully experiencing what is right in front of us instead of living in a make believe world of what ifs. Presence and acceptance go hand-in-hand. And if we know that a lack of acceptance equals suffering, then we can surmise that a lack of presence also equals suffering. I love you.

Month
7

January 10

Life can seem like too much to handle when we forget we are souls having a human experience. That all is in order—the purpose of life is to experience the juxtaposition of joy and pain, love and heartbreak. The hard stuff, the heartbreak, is not an accident. These moments break us wide open and are our greatest teachers. They guide us to take new paths that we wouldn't have seen otherwise. They break us down to our core: love. Nothing matters or makes sense after a tragedy except for love. When it all feels like too much, try to remember that you are an eternal, loving soul who is connected to it all. Keep coming back to this knowing, and see if it's possible to be grateful for it all. I love you.

January 11

Today I attended a breathwork and yoga retreat. We did an activity
that I've done before and think that everyone should do to help
you to live consciously. It's to write your own eulogy. Now, imagine
what life and legacy you want to create in this life and compare
it to where you currently put your energy. In many eulogies, we
talk about the family we've created as well as our jobs, degrees,
and hobbies. Today, when I wrote my eulogy, I realized that it's
my hope that the love, passion, and heart that people felt in my
presence makes all of the other stuff insignificant. That there's not
enough time to talk about my superficial accomplishments because
there are too many stories of people feeling better after having
encountered me.

January 12

Acceptance is the key to being able to continue living after a massive loss. I said right after Noah transitioned that I will never, and can never, accept his death or never seeing him again. That will never happen. I can, however, accept that I have to work on creating a new relationship with him in his spirit form. Acceptance isn't accepting death as many envision it. It's remembering and accepting that life doesn't end with physical death. That consciousness and energy doesn't die. Acceptance is realizing that we have to live consciously on Earth to be able to connect with our spirit family. We have to slow down, raise our vibration to try to reach theirs, quiet the mind, and intentionally connect. Look for and be open to the signs. To feel their love and energy. This is an acceptance that changes the way I live my life for the better. It's an acceptance I can try to live with.

January 13

It's all okay. I know this. Because I know that the struggles are the point. And that even after the worst thing we can imagine happens—a loved one leaves us by physically dying—they are okay. And we can choose to stay in that knowing and reduce our human suffering in the midst of all of the hard stuff. When I start to feel overwhelmed, one of the tools I use to help me regain a state where I can function is to zoom out on my life. I zoom all of the way out to look at the Earth from space ... knowing Noah exists in a dimension right next to me, but where I can't see him with my 3D human eyes or hear him with my limited frequency human ears. Zoom out, and the things we think are huge are really not. Zoom out, and see things from the soul perspective. I feel that if I can do this after my child transitioned, then I can do this with anything in life—everything else pales in comparison and will feel far easier. Zoom out. It is all okay. I love you.

January 14

I can read a book, listen to a podcast, go to therapy, meditate, have a meaningful conversation, and as a result I sense the "ahas." To have a sense of knowing and understanding that makes life feel tolerable. And then just as soon as I have that, the next day it can be gone. I can be back to feeling massive existential dread, wondering what the point of it all is. I've realized that this awakening is a lifestyle. I need to bathe myself in it daily. I need to surround myself with those on the same journey. I need consistent reminders of my soul and spirituality. This is what builds my foundation, solidifies my knowing, helps me to consciously show up to connect with other humans, my spirit family, and my higher self. This is what I want to offer to the world, and in doing so what will save me.

January 15

Today was full of emotion. Evidence that Noah is watching over us every day. I am emotionally exhausted and so grateful to him for showing up so strongly. More to come once I've had an opportunity to process it all. Thank you, Noah. I love you.

January 16

Yesterday I had an amazing session with a medium who brought Noah through loud and clear. I was so excited and nervous for this session. I've been on a wait list for months and have been waiting in anxious anticipation to connect. Hoping that this medium was legitimate. Hoping that Noah's vibration would match hers and she could pick up on his signals. Noah sends me signs frequently, and I'm working on my ability to communicate with him better by myself, but this provided an opportunity to have an objective experience with undeniable proof that his spirit continues to exist and is present in our lives. While Noah came through without a doubt, I felt an interesting mix of heaviness and lightness after the reading. It was wonderful to connect with him, and to know that he is all good. But this was likely the closest I will be to him in terms of communication, but I long for more. And this is where the heaviness remains. I will long for him to be in my life the way he was, likely forever. I have a huge part of my heart that is with him always. It's a visceral feeling of missing a part of me. I can focus on that, or I can focus on continuing to build this new relationship with him. A relationship that intellectually I know is even closer than when he was in his body. And being grateful for the ache in my heart that is my love and eternal connection to him.

January 17

Love is my religion. I have a bumper sticker on my altar for Noah that says these words. The bumper sticker arrived in the mail a few days after Noah transitioned; he had just ordered it for himself. Bob Marley became one of our favorites when living on the boat, and Noah had recently taken an interest in Ziggy Marley's music. I keep these words on his altar because I love that Noah vibed with that idea, but also because it's what became crystal clear after Noah's transition. My life is centered on love. For myself. For others. And for something greater. I love you.

January 18

Today, I'm grateful for friends who I can be real with. And who are real right back. I see and understand how hard it is for people to know how to be or what to say. I get it. I think the best we can do is to be real, even if it's saying, "I don't know what to say or how to act, but I really care."

January 19

It seems that I have come to know of many "tragedies" (or what I'm coming to know as regularly occurring, but very difficult to accept, life events) as of late, and as I was thinking about another one this morning. I thought about the phrase "my heart aches for you." I was feeling that for a particular person and their family, and then I recognized that feeling in my chest. In my heart. And it was a heart bursting with love and compassion. I have said before how it's hard for me to be around people who look at me with such sadness. I understand they care deeply and that is why their response holds so much heaviness. I've also talked multiple times about how love and pain coexist and are two sides of the same coin. You can't have one without the other, and sometimes it's hard to differentiate between the two. What if instead of responding to someone drowning in their own pain with more sadness, we responded with how much love and compassion we have for them. What if we focused on that instead of the ache or broken heart? Just like I try to redirect my intense pain during my fits of grief to my love and gratitude for Noah. Consider consciously trying to acknowledge love over everything else. It won't take away the pain, but it offers us a buoy to hold on to when we feel like we're drowning.

January 20

Noah looks so much like my dad in this picture. So handsome. I just want to kiss those cheeks! In the heaviness of this grief, I have wanted to protect and take away as much pain as I can from Grant and Hope. My heart is exploding for them—wishing I could do the work for them so they didn't have to struggle. And then I look at my own process, and I realize that no one can take away my pain or work through this for me; it's a gift, and I have to trust my own higher self to be there for my human self. To trust in myself that I will find my way. That I will be open to those people and opportunities sent to help me. If that's the case for me, that is also the case for my kiddos. My work is not to take it away but to help them realize that their higher self is there whenever they need it, how to access it, and that they are not alone, even when it might sometimes feel like it as a human. I love you.

January 21

I am reading *The Power of Now* by Eckhart Tolle and had a huge light bulb go off today. A reminder that light is the only way to get rid of the darkness. We all have a pain body. It's the part of us that surfaces when we are threatened emotionally. It gets triggered by human interactions and minds. It's the dark gloominess, the despair, the depression, the anger ... some bury it away and it only sometimes rears its ugly head. Some live with it on the surface. But we all have it to some degree. Our ego minds identify with it. "I'm alone, I'm sad, I'm abandoned, I'm worthless, I'm not good enough, etc." We think we are our emotions (which are created by our thoughts). When we ignore the pain body, it often comes out through physical ailments. When ignored, it feeds on and gets bigger through interactions that continue these feelings, often leading to us subconsciously put ourselves in situations that continue to feed the monster and these dark emotions. How do we deal with this pain body so that we can be free of it and reduce our suffering? We must acknowledge the emotions instead of ignoring them. And see ourselves as separate from them. Become the watcher of the emotions. Become aware that our perception is everything and we can and do create our own emotional suffering through our thoughts. By consciously being aware of and watching our dark emotions, it shines a light on them. Darkness can't survive the light—it becomes the light. Choice. Presence. Perception. Zooming out. Knowing we are not our thoughts or emotions. This is how we continue in our human form with the least amount of suffering. This is not easy stuff. There is a motto in the support group I've become a part of: We are not bereaved parents; we are shining light parents. The goodness and light of our children shine through us. This is a choice. It's a perception. We acknowledge our pain, witness it, and know that we are so much more than our pain, and our children are so much more than their physical death. I love you.

January 22

Time. If you knew you had six months to live, how would you spend your time? This thought is what prompted our move onto the boat that we named "Dessert First." We realized we were not guaranteed tomorrow and wanted to get out of the rat race and really "live" rather than shuttle our kids to school, work eight hours, shuttle them back, dinner, bath, bed, repeat. I have been contemplating this thought again the past few days, so this is me thinking aloud … should we live life based on time ticking away or just focus on each present moment, appreciating and finding joy even in the mundane? If we live focused on what our plans are for the future (none of which is guaranteed, not even the six months), then are we taking ourselves out of the present? What a gift time gives us in allowing us to reflect on what is important and what we want to put our focus and attention on. Without the concept of time, we may not have this reason for reflection and intention. What if "really living" is just about spreading love with everyone you come in contact with? About intensely loving those special to you? In each moment that we have the opportunity. While I still love adventuring and travel, I've realized the focus I want is on spending quality time with and meaningfully interacting with those I love. On a boat or at home. I think the main difference is prioritizing quality time with loved ones. It was easier to have quality time together on the boat. But in "regular" life, can we get rid of as many commitments that don't add meaning to your life and take away opportunities for meaningful connection? Restructuring everyday life intentionally so that connection is always the first priority. Living each day as if we're dying (because we are all one day closer to death today), gives us the motivation to live consciously and intentionally. Once again, I'm convinced that death is our greatest teacher. A gift. It exists for a reason. I love you.

January 23

I found a box of Noah's artwork the other day. I love seeing the creations from his brain. Our Noah wisdom for today: Be Chill, like a jellyfish with an umbrella.

January 24

I keep working on the eulogy that I hope is said at my celebration of life. I am not quite there yet, but this exercise gives me direction, focus, and inspiration for the person I want to be.

Tiffany was a passionate lover of life. She felt deeply and gave all of herself to those she loved and those she felt she could positively impact. Upon her physical death, we know she was anxiously anticipating and was excited to transition to spirit form to see her sweet Noah again. She has assured those of us left behind that she will remain ever present and protective. Her teaching and insights into life are forever gifted to us through her writings and time spent listening and working with others trying to find their way in this life and beyond. Her greatest joy has been watching her children grow, learn, and thrive. While she loved adventuring, traveling, and creating, in the second half of her life, she realized and demonstrated the power of the basics—presence, love, and connection—and she poured that into everyone around her. Her essence is that of pure love and compassion. We felt that when she was with us on Earth, and we continue to feel it today.

I love you.

January 25

Six months ago today, Noah transitioned from his body into spirit form. He left his troubled mind behind. Those of us who spend a lot of time in the health and wellness arena understand how hormones influence our emotions. And our hormones are created by the brain, the mind. Our mind is influenced and at times controlled by many factors—our natural hormone production related to our age/biology, reaction to societal pressures, relationships, outside substances (legal and not legal), music, social media, physical struggles, etc. Our mind can be a great partner to our soul, but it can also be our worst enemy. We have to understand that we are separate from our mind. We have to give our mind all of the things to help it be a great partner and avoid the things that make it our worst enemy. We can only restrict our exposure to things that are not good for the mind to a degree. And so we have to understand in our brains and hearts that we have the power to reduce our suffering through not only managing external influences but also KNOWING that we have the power to choose how we perceive EVERYTHING. I reflect on this major life lesson for how I wish I had been able to help Noah with this more, and also as a major lesson for how I am now dealing with my grief. This is a struggle for many—kids, teens, and adults. It is hard to say, "I see death as a gift" instead of, "Death is the worst thing that could ever happen." It is hard to say, "I see love in and have love for every soul I encounter" instead of, "That person makes me feel like shit, I can't stand them, and I can't forgive them." It is hard to say, "I deserve love and compassion" instead of, "I'm not good enough, I don't deserve goodness." It is hard but necessary if we want to live a life based on more love and less struggle. And at its core, this is what Noah keeps telling me … Be Chill. Love is my religion. Nothing is permanent. Spirit and energy live on. There is no death. Fear is our own human construct. Noah, I miss hugging you, hearing your thoughts and jokes, watching you grow. And I am so thankful for our new relationship. Nothing stays the same. We are ever evolving.

January 26

Noah's favorite thing was for me to run my finger between his eyebrows from his nose up to his forehead. It helped him relax and go to sleep. He even let me do it as he got older when he needed some extra loving. When Hope was a baby, he did that for her, too. I've been thinking a lot about how to help parents help their children. So many kids are going through either just the normal social and hormonal challenges of growing up, which 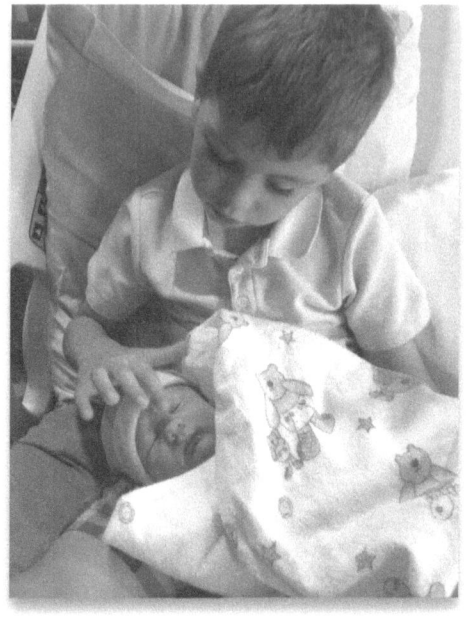 are extremely hard in their own right, or real anxiety, depression, and dread. It can feel so overwhelming as a parent, trying to figure out how best to help. We have been gifted the great responsibility of guiding these autonomous souls on their journeys. We need to start talking to each other and making this a priority. While I obviously couldn't save Noah—there was a perfect storm of factors that I believe contributed to this outcome—I do believe there are many things that we CAN do to help give our kids the tools to not just get through life, but thrive and grow in leaps and bounds while doing it. I have been thinking about this, researching it, and practicing it with my Earth-side kids every single day for the past six months.

January 27

Today I am missing Noah's smile, laugh, and playful energy so much. This weekend I was thinking about how even when I turn my focus away from sorrow and focus instead on my intense love and gratitude for Noah, my heart feels constricted. It can physically hurt and feel like my chest is going to explode as I move from feeling sorrow to love. It's a better feeling than it being ripped apart by sorrow, but still not one that feels sustainable or ideal. I am still very much protecting my heart from a place of fear. I think it's a fear of feeling too much. I haven't been able to physically open my heart—the literal act of opening my arms up and spreading my arms out to expose my heart sounds scary. Even moving my body in any big way (dancing, yoga, lifting weights) feels scary. I know the enormous and infinite amount of love that is inside of me, and it's scary to open my heart completely to it. I'm not sure I can even articulate why, but tears flow when I imagine it. Not necessarily sad tears, but overwhelmed tears. Do you know that feeling you have after a big cry? When you feel an overwhelming calm and ease in your body? That is what I'm aiming for now when I think about my love and gratitude for this amazing soul and the gift of his life as a part of mine. Instead of gripping onto my love as a source of survival, I want to let it flow with ease. I want to feel it all around me. I want to be able to open my heart completely. I want to express it fully without fear and limits. I want to trust that all is okay. That once I am able to fully express my own divine love in human form I will be in alignment, and I can handle whatever comes with that. I love you.

January 28

Love and Fear versus Love and Trust. When you love someone so incredibly much, you might feel a fear of something bad happening to them or losing them. You will do whatever it takes to keep them safe and to help them when they are in need. And sometimes that is out of your control. Sometimes there are outside factors that you can't change. Sometimes the help you want to provide is not accessible, and that can feel maddening. There is a lesson in this for me as Noah's physical death was not the only scenario in which I'm being challenged in this area. Surrender. Trust. Knowing we are a part of something bigger. These are the opposite of fear, control, and attachment. We can do everything in our power, and have to give the rest up to the Universe. To trust that all is okay and as it should be. Even when it feels like it's the furthest thing from okay. I'm practicing intentional action coming from a place of love. And then surrender and trust. I love you.

January 29

I've been reflecting on a passage in *The Power of Now* about actual time (all we have is now—literally this very moment is all that exists) versus psychological time (thinking about the past and future). Tolle talks about how psychological time is the form of mental illness most prominent as humans—it's insanity and suffering-making when we live in the past or in projections of the future. Which is where our minds live the majority of the time unless we make a concerted effort to be totally present in the moment. And none of the reminiscing or projecting matters or is real in the only reality we have, which is now. This made me laugh because it's so true, so simple, and yet it's so hard for us to see. Sure, we have goals and life situations for which we need to figure out the next step, but none of that is reality ... yet. Maybe it never will be. That, coupled with knowing that life is eternal, that even if the thing we've labeled/perceived as the worst thing that could ever happen, happens (e.g. us or someone else we love dying), it will all be okay. That all is good, no matter what. This week as I notice myself living in past situations or imagining future situations, I have been snapping myself back by saying, "Now." But in a really long and drawn out way. Because the second I say *now*, it's gone and there's a new now. It's always *nooooooowwwww*. (Credit to my friend Anna Marie Enea for that gem.) I love you.

January 30

I have been keeping the families of the passengers on the aircraft that crashed last night in my heart. Knowing what those first moments of shock and terror feel like when you find out about a very sudden, unexpected, and horrific outcome. Knowing that nothing will ever be the same. You have experienced a lifequake like no other. You have been broken to the core and will have to find a way to rebuild, but rebuilding is not even in the periphery of your thoughts. You are thrust into the present moment like no other, at least for those initial moments. The work is to stay there instead of reliving the past and what could have been different or thinking about the future you thought you'd have, but won't. The work is to understand this human life and our soul's work. I've come to realize that each person has to work through their trauma and grief on their own, in their own time. The process of making this decision is part of the journey. They need to decide if it will be an opportunity for growth or not. Nobody can tell them that it is. And if/when they decide that growth is a part of not only their survival, but their ability to thrive in a way that would not have been possible before, I want to be there to help. This is Post Traumatic Growth and it's the foundation of the work I intend to offer to the world. Big love to all those suffering right now. I see you.

January 31

Anger is really based in fear. It bubbles up when you feel threatened and out of control. It would be easy to stay in anger—it's not fair what happened, it's not fair that the fallout in my life after Noah's death has happened, I'm scared of the future, I'm scared I won't make it, I'm scared of bad things continuing to happen to people I love. These thoughts can effortlessly enter my head. It feels heavy and constricted in my body and heart. It's hard work to change my perspective in these moments. But it IS a choice to change my perspective. I've come to understand that my anger is spurred by unmet expectations. And my fear is spurred by a lack of presence and knowing. When I let go of my attachment to expectations from certain people or of this life in general, and I ground myself in knowing that all is well and in divine order, that my children (Noah included) and I are good, right now, in this present moment, I can feel a sense of lightness, softness, and ease in my body. This is my work. Everyday. I love you.

February 1

Soul Work and Social Work. I have spent my life volunteering; as a kid in school to become a social worker and as a social work professional. I got into social work because I was passionate about justice and helping change systems so that all people could have access to what they need to live a healthy and safe life. To me, social work was about how the larger systems impact the individual (top down). Somehow, along the way, social work has begun to focus on individual therapy and lost its focus on systems (bottom up). Instead we are stuck in the medical model, working with insurance systems and struggling to make the change we want to with clients and in the world. We struggle because many of us have limited our view of how we work with people. We work to help people problem solve and learn tools to help manage living in a society that is not healthy. We suggest prescription medications to mask the root cause of our discontent and suffering. Many of us have forgotten that our brains are not the same as our soul. I see so much value in folks helping us manage living in this world that we can't change overnight. We need that for survival and to even begin to think about Soul Work. But we can't stop at learning how to function in life without crumbling. We need to address how we thrive and create large-scale change. In my grief journey, I've realized that light can only take out darkness. That masking only extends suffering. That we have to get to the root. That personal work translates to society in a ripple effect. That doing Soul Work is how we can improve our communities in the long term. Soul Work is Post Traumatic Growth. It's expanding our light. I used to see things from the top down, and in my time working in social policy, I quickly realized that we have very little lasting influence in that world. And it's often a dark battle. I've revised my approach to bottom up. But true bottom—not surface/human brain level individual work—but deep Soul Work. This is how I see the world shifting more toward the light. I love you.

February 2

I had an epiphany last night. I feel like they are happening almost everyday. I have been working through the purpose of life and our role in the Universe and beyond. And I've also been trying to understand the very human lessons I'm supposed to be learning from this trauma. I don't think I realized until last night, that knowing our purpose for being here—our soul's plan, that everything is love, light snuffs out darkness, time does not exist, death is not to be feared, we create our reality, we are not our mind, we are all one, etc.—all of these truths and knowing make it so we can better see and learn from our human lessons. They awaken us so that we can learn. Otherwise, we are walking around deeply unconscious and just bouncing from human challenge to human challenge wondering why the world is so hard and cruel so much of the time. I accidentally drove past the house where I discovered Noah's body last night. I have actively been avoiding it. I quickly went straight back to that day. That day on the lawn I remember wailing, "My baby," "I'm sorry," "I'm so deeply sorry" over and over again. I have traced my actions from the moment I knew I was pregnant with him until the day he took his life. There are many things I wish I could have done differently. Many. I know one of my human lessons in this is to see everyone as part of the same universal love, including myself. I think I am supposed to be working through guilt and shame to understand self-compassion. To understand self-compassion, I have to experience the opposite. That I could not save my child. That I made mistakes. And compassion and forgiveness for others, who made mistakes and were a part of the perfect storm that took Noah's physical life. When I understand that I am here to learn from the duality that Earth provides, it makes it possible to zoom out and really understand on a cellular level that Noah's death was also a part of my life plan. He gave that gift to me (us) to learn and grow. Thank you, Noah. I love you.

February 3

I remember the day this photo was taken. We were just getting started exploring the Bahamas. We anchored in a new bay and wanted to explore underwater. We kayaked and swam in the late afternoon until the sun started setting. There wasn't much to see, but Noah found this shell and dove deep to get it.

We brought it back to the boat and it contained a living occupant, so we put it back in the ocean. I love how brave and adventurous this kid is. One of the many reasons I admire him. I hadn't been down to Noah's room for six months. I just couldn't be in his space. Where he was just before he decided to take his life. To see his bed, unslept in. See/smell his clothes, his muddy soccer cleats, snowboard gear. But after the session with the medium, where Noah came through so clearly, something changed. I don't know what exactly, because I already felt him around. I knew he was okay and present in our lives. But after that session, I went downstairs and cleaned up his room. I felt an urge to nest. I wanted to make it cozy. A place we could go and feel good. I moved his bed so that there was more natural light and I moved my meditation cushion and other things right in front of the window. I've been spending time down there most mornings. I get to be in his energy. And for the first time I'm not scared of it. I'm embracing it. Finding calm in it. Noah told me through the medium that he doesn't want me to think of or relive his death. There is nothing good that comes from that. He didn't say this part, but I know that reliving his death is living in the past, which no longer exists. We are in the present, and in the present he's just a breath, a thought away. He still exists— inside of me and in the Universe. This is why I'm working so hard on helping my brain and nervous system release this trauma. This reliving is involuntary in the form of flashbacks and panic attacks. It adds another layer of difficulty to post traumatic growth. I want to be able to focus on my love, sorrow, and new relationship with and for Noah. With Noah's help, I'm finding my way. I love you.

February 4

Noah found these glasses thrifting in Bangkok. He could pull off any style. Another thing I admired about him. I really loved hanging out with him. I was so looking forward to the day we could be friends. I consciously built a big family, having three kids, because between dysfunctional relationships and early deaths, I have always felt like I didn't have a family. I always envied those with big families, especially those that got along  and were supportive of each other. My little nuclear family was/is my everything. Noah's physical departure has felt like a massive loss in general, but also another reminder that it doesn't matter what I do, I can't count on anyone staying around. Attachment is suffering. That I am ultimately alone. We all are really. We are born, live, and die with ourselves. We need to like ourselves, love ourselves, nurture ourselves, trust ourselves. Time spent connecting with ourselves is often overlooked or put as a last priority. This lifetime is teaching me that both connection with others and with ourselves are of equal importance. We are one. Connection with others is hugely important, but a connection with yourself is just as important. Connection with nature and something higher eases some of the loneliness too. When I'm feeling down, I can connect with myself deeply and spend time in nature ... this is likc a balm for my soul when I feel disconnected from myself and others.

February 5

We are responsible for the energy we emit to the world. Even when we're in the midst of darkness or chaos, our energy matters. I was reminded of this last week as I was pulled into the darkness: My energy impacts those around me. When I saw this in action, it pulled me out of it. I don't want to negatively impact those around me if I'm capable of shifting my perspective and energy. I can help by adding light or hinder by adding darkness. If someone's energetic battery is low, they will need to draw on a high energy battery. We can't always be the high energy battery, but we should be consciously aware that we should be when we can be. We can light the way for those experiencing hardships behind us, just as we look to those who have lit the way for us.

February 6

I'm a thinker. I used to stay in my head and had a hard time not letting my mind control everything. For the longest time I didn't know how to listen to my gut, my heart, my intuition. My mind would constantly get in the way. This loss has made me search for answers to many, many questions. There are so many different takes on suicide, life after death, forgiveness, life's purpose, etc. I have had to figure out how to determine what my truth is. And the very simple way I have found to do that is to listen solely to my body. If I think of a perspective and it hurts my stomach or heart, then it is not my truth. If it feels easy, soft and calm in my body, then it sits right with my soul. If it evokes emotion and tears associated with love and gratitude, then it sits right with my soul. For example, if I think about death being a punishment, the forever end, and it makes me want to die, then my concept of death is not right. If I shift my perspective higher, zooming out, think about an eternal soul and purpose from suffering from human death—I feel calm and at ease. And so much gratitude for all of it. Thank you, Noah. I love you.

February 7

How would your life change if you felt every challenge was an opportunity created and chosen by your higher self for growth? That a life without challenge is a life without growth? What if you knew that the people and situations that cause you the most grief are in your life as a gift? That it's all part of a beautiful plan? To learn from the duality we have on Earth—to understand the depths of our love and compassion that cannot be understood without great loss. I truly believe that Noah and I (and others seismically impacted by his early departure) planned this before we incarnated. To help us grow and learn. Noah's life and physical death have been the biggest gift I've been given in life. He gave that to me because of our deep love and connection. He gave me the gift of being shaken awake, to understand and know myself, to have a depth of compassion and empathy for others that is not possible without this experience. He has shown me the way to work through this so that I can shine a light for others that will walk this dark path. I have felt that I don't want to "waste" this grief, but just yesterday I had this knowing even deeper. To honor this gift Noah has given me, I need to keep doing the deep Soul Work and following the path being presented, and that I feel in my gut the desire to help others trying to figure out how to survive and thrive after a lifequake. I show my love for and honor Noah's gift to me in this way. Thank you, Noah. I love you.

February 8

Being a parent is the biggest challenge I have experienced. There have been moments where I have questioned my ability to be the parent that my kids need. That maybe I shouldn't have had kids, because I have been ill-prepared for the task. It's so scary to want the best for your kids and sometimes not know how to give that to them. In my spiritual inquiry, I've been given a new appreciation for the challenges in life. I've realized that not knowing all of the answers might be just what our kids need to learn their own Earth school lessons and grow. I've realized that my role in their life isn't to make it perfect. It's to love them through the mess and try to guide them in how to navigate the mess. To provide them opportunities for joy. To honor their own life lived in the duality of Earth. And to know that part of that mess is being an imperfect parent. My kids are my greatest teachers. They have taught me a love that I never would have known. They have been mirrors for me in my own challenges and growth. In my quest for self-compassion, my therapist would often ask me if I would treat my kids the way I treat myself. It has taught me to use my depth of love for them to learn how to love myself. They have reminded me when I needed to find my grounded center again. They have shown me the importance of compassion, acceptance, and devotion. They are wise in their own right. While I understand it's my role to help guide them, I also honor and see their own unique soul's contributions to my life and learning. I believe we chose each other for a reason. I am so grateful for all my kids have taught me. And the depth of love their existence has made possible in my heart.

February 9

Compassion vs. pity: I've experienced this from others, but am also realizing how I entertain these two ways of being in relation to myself. Self-compassion vs self-pity. Pity is devoid of respect, of faith, of hope, of empathy. It is a harsh feeling to be on the receiving end of pity. Pity is to look at someone as if they are other than you, as if their life challenge could never touch you. As if their life challenge is only ugly and does not contain beauty. It is a false and limited, surface-level sense of reality. Compassion is love. It is seeing our interconnectedness and feeling the sorrow and love together. To feel another's challenges deeply. It is acknowledging the messiness and challenge of life and saying, I see you. I have deep challenges too. And we are in this human experience together. It is acknowledging that all of our lives are imperfect and beautiful at the same time. That we are the same, not different. It's being real. I love you.

Month
8

February 10

When Noah transitioned, I immediately wondered what I had done in this life or a past life to deserve the fate of losing a child, especially to suicide. I assumed it had to be karma—how else could something this awful happen to a mother? I scanned my life searching for a reason I deserved this. I researched all there was to know about karma, karmic debts, past lives ... and what I've determined is that, yes, there was a reason for this. And that it did likely have to do with karma. But not in the way we think about karma. I've concluded that karma is a *this, then that* law. A law of give and take—but for everyone's good—not as a punishment. Perhaps in a past life I sacrificed my life early to help Noah understand a life lesson, and he and I made an agreement that he would help me with the same in this life. I don't know a lot. I'm doing my best to understand this life and what I'm supposed to get out of it. Meaning-making is my salvation. And I wholeheartedly believe that the purpose of this life is not to behave and be perfect or be punished. I believe all of our experiences—the tragedies and the exhilarations are all there for our greater good. Karma is not a bitch. Karma is a gift. I love you.

February 11

I learned a while back that the biological reason for crying is to calm the nervous system. Our tears contain cortisol, the stress hormone, and regulate our systems by expelling the built up emotional energy. I didn't used to be a big crier, but the tears seem to flow effortlessly now. When I think of my deep love and appreciation for my loves, when I think of our struggles and the hard work that we are doing to survive and thrive, they fall from my eyes without any resistance. I've realized that crying is a super power. It's like a bath for the soul. When we hold our emotions inside, it builds and builds, ultimately locking our grief in place. When we cry, it washes away the pain to a tolerable level for the present moment. Over time, instead of it building up layers, we can fully feel the present-moment pain instead of all of the years of pain piled and crusted on top of each other. To heal, we need the full expression of pain. To fully feel. Tears keep energy flowing. Can we allow crying and expression to be natural and spontaneous? To normalize this instead of hiding it or being embarrassed? To allow it for people in our presence instead of cowering away or running from expression. Allowing yourself the time and space to cry, to fully feel, is self-compassion. And allowing others to do this in your presence is a wonderful example of compassion. Can we treat ourselves like a friend and comfort and hold space for our tearful expression of emotion?

February 12

Growing up, my dad would always talk about how if we didn't like someone's behavior, then they were a mirror for something we didn't like in ourselves. He would say that our reaction to someone is our own, and it has nothing to do with them. I never really understood this concept. My reaction was always that I was the opposite of that person and that's why I didn't like them—we definitely didn't have anything in common. That I felt a certain way because of their faults. Not my own. I'm seeing now that my own lack of self-compassion is mirrored in my lack of compassion for others. My need for others to be perfect is mirrored in my need to be perfect. My need to be perfect is rooted in my feelings of inadequacy. My feelings of inadequacy stem from deep wounds given to me at an early age by those that also felt inadequate, imperfect, and lacked self-compassion. It's all a big mirror. A big cycle. And I'm finally awake enough to see it. To stop it, so that the cycle doesn't continue. Once you can see your mirrors clearly, you've found the golden ticket. The prize that offers entrance into a deeper understanding and growth. This may seem tangentially related to my grief, but I believe this is one of the great gifts Noah has given me. To take my experience of deep and unconditional love and acceptance for and from my kids and to use that as a guide for how to love myself and others. Thank you Noah. I love you.

February 13

I had a small breakthrough yesterday: Sometimes we fight our whole lives to resist the things we don't want to be, feel, or accept. But what if the first step in the process of changing is to lean into the reality we are resisting? I've been battling many feelings and realities. Feeling weak and guilty, like I could crawl into the fetal position and never come out. I have been resisting by being *strong* and *capable*, taking care of others, still attempting to contribute and feel of value. I was encouraged to let myself fall into my current feelings instead of fighting them. This is similar to a concept in bodywork called positional release. The pain will subside if you just let your body fall into the position that feels natural. If you rest there long enough with the intention of not staying there forever, but giving in for a moment to let the body reset naturally, the pain point often releases. Stretching in the opposite direction, deep pressure, or trying to force the release often makes it worse. So, I'm going to try to allow myself to fall into my current emotional struggles instead of creating so much rigid resistance in both my mind and body to be "better" or redeem myself in some way. Step by step. Some things can't be rushed or forced. Just like my tears, I will try to let this process flow as it needs to, knowing I don't have all of the answers.

February 14

As I'm learning more about my soul and my invisible, conscious presence as separate from my mind and body, I've been wondering more about the role of the body. What is its purpose outside of carrying us around to learn our Earth school lessons? While I have felt so disconnected from my body at intense times during this trauma, I have also noticed it is a powerful emotional communicator. It has felt scary and unsafe to be in my body at times. I still really am only conscious of my body when I notice its expression of emotions such as pain, anxiety, fear, love, gratitude, etc. My professional work has been around the mind-body connection, and yet, I'm realizing that it's not as simple as what I've been teaching. Maybe the important piece goes just beyond disconnecting the mind from the body, but to then connect with the soul housed inside of the body. Our minds are the crazy-making machines, telling us stories, creating fear, taking us out of the present moment, etc. But when we turn off the mind and focus on what is housed inside of our physical shell, we can feel our essence, our light energy, our soul, our vibration. That is where we can find calm, ease, and presence. Here is a quote from Eckhart Tolle about connecting with the inner body that made me laugh out loud because of how insane and accurate it is:

"But that is only the beginning of an inward journey that will take you ever more deeply into a realm of great stillness and peace, yet also of great power and vibrant life. At first, you may only get fleeting glimpses of it, but through them you will begin to realize that you are not just a meaningless fragment in an alien universe, briefly suspended between birth and death, allowed a few short-lived pleasures followed by pain and ultimate annihilation. Underneath your outer form, you are connected with something so vast, so immeasurable and sacred, that it cannot be conceived of."

February 15

Noah and Grant were only twenty months apart, so it was really like having two babies at once. As two babies, they couldn't exactly be emotionally close for a bit, but they grew to be so close as they got older, especially during our time on the boat and Covid when they relied heavily on each other. I've been wondering how to best guide Grant and Hope through this lifequake and loss of their big brother given that they aren't likely to read the books I'm reading, listen to the podcasts I'm listening to, engage in the groups I'm a part of, or even be open to the alternative therapies that I'm exploring. I want to help them navigate this, but often feel at a loss. I mentioned this during a Helping Parents Heal meeting today, and one of the parents said we just have to lead by example. It made me think about the little things lately that they seem to notice or pick up on. Sometimes they tease me about being woo-woo, but I think it's making them think. Opening their eyes to a different way of seeing grief, life, and death. To explore some of these existential questions on their own. And sometimes they come to conclusions on their own that help me and change my perspective. Hope once said, with the innocence and practicality of a child, "I don't understand why everyone is so upset—he's still here. I feel him all of the time." I tearfully laughed when she said that because she sees so clearly what the rest of us have trouble seeing through our programmed narratives about death. What a gift Noah has given them to be able to reflect and come to their own "knowings" at such a young age— to find their own foundation and go deep now—in a way that will impact how they live their lives forever.

February 16

Noah and I went jet skiing in San Diego, and he humored me as I shrieked at each wave going 20 mph or less. The kid who went 65 mph down the mountain said this was boring. As I think more about our human bodies I realize that they are also our main communicator from our soul to our brains (the opposite, brain to the soul, is where we get in trouble). Our bodies are so sensitive and let us know if we are in alignment with the divine nature of our soul. When we are unconsciously walking around, sometimes we forget we have bodies, let alone souls. But when we listen to them, they tell us what the next right decision is with either a constriction and heaviness or with a lightness, ease, and excitement. If we are solely in our minds then we use logic, pro/con lists, materialistic objectives, etc. to help us make our decisions. When we are in our bodies, we use our intuition and inner "knowing." For a very long time I could not feel my intuition. I had trouble identifying what my body was telling me. But I think it's because my mind was getting in the way. It would create a story out of fear and my body would listen to that; thus, creating the heaviness or constriction. When we take that pesky mind out of the equation, we can hear our soul through our body.

February 17

I've been thinking a lot about the feeling of hope and its relationship to attachment. Hope feels essential to any movement out of depression—we must believe that it won't always be this way. That things change and can change for the better. That we won't always feel the suffering we do now. But if we have hope, are we attaching to an outcome? Attachment that if the outcome is not delivered, will lead to more suffering? I've come to the conclusion that there is no way up and out of the despair unless there is some glimmer of hope on the horizon. That hope can come in many forms. Hope for me comes from my knowing that Noah is still alive, that we are eternal beings, that this life is just a blip in time, and we will gain much from enduring its lessons. Hope is not that nothing "bad" will happen again. Or that I won't lose anyone important to me again. Or even that my heart won't feel broken for the rest of my life. It's simply that the brokenness is meaningful. And that the suffering illuminates how much I have and continue to love. I believe that in this version of hope, I don't have an attachment to a specific outcome, which is sure to create more suffering. But instead, my hope is in the more overarching meaning to life. A friend of mine reminded me of the scale of emotion recently. It shows hope at the precipice of all of the other higher vibration emotions. It's the gateway to non-suffering. Noah Grants Hope. I love you.

February 18

Today I am tired.

And hopeful.

And knowing that the waves between being exhausted from surviving and being hopeful that we'll get through it are consistent and somewhat predictable makes feeling both at the same time possible.

February 19

I've heard several times from different sources to get rid of the word "should" from your vocabulary. I have to admit that I have noticed I've used it more than once in relation to how we address mental health, think about parenting, being conscious, etc.

I suppose the word to take its place could be "consider." We are all unique beings who respond differently to stimuli, approaches, ways of thinking, etc.

I've had to open my brain from the societal expectations for my reaction to my son's physical death, to being open and considering different realities/approaches. This consideration has been my salvation. This opening of the mind and heart to thoughts of acceptance versus resistance, love versus blame, holding space for multiple realities to be true at the same time. Because nothing is black and white (a lesson I've been trying to learn for many years).

May we consider, be open, and flow with what feels helpful and right in our soul.

I love you.

February 20

I was interviewed for the *Beyond the Dose* podcast to talk about radical acceptance last month. The episode came out today and I took a listen. My brain is often in a fog, and I didn't really even remember what I said.

I'm feeling quite emotional after hearing myself talk about my journey. Little things like this reflected back to me make the reality of my situation hit home. It's something concrete out in the world saying that I lost my son to suicide. It might sound odd because I write about it every day, but there are some days I walk through life knowing it in the back of my head but having to function anyway. And then there are moments when I get a reality check. They aren't infrequent, but some hit you over the head just a little bit harder than others.

I don't want this to be my identity; however, at the moment it is consuming me. And I feel passionately about sharing my discoveries about life, death, meaning-making, and post traumatic growth. Noah has gifted me with a life-altering experience by being his parent and the intense contrast of losing that role in his life. I believe his passing is meant to help others, and at times he is using me as a vessel for that to happen. I hope you take a listen and some part of it touches you in a way that makes a difference in your life.

I love you.

February 21

Yesterday I had a follow-up mammogram. They led me into a quiet room, gave me a warm blanket, water, and sat down to tell me what my original scans showed and what the potential outcomes would be after this second scan.

I was a little nervous. I have been actively working to improve my health so that I can be here for as long as I can to help support my Earth-side kiddos. The way they were interacting with me made me feel like this was maybe more serious than I thought.

I waited in the quiet room after my scans—the doctor would read them immediately to let me know what path I would need to walk down. And when the kind woman walked in with a big smile to tell me it was door #1 and I was all clear, I sobbed. And then I sobbed more when I realized why I was sobbing. The imaging tech thought I was emotional because of relief, but it was an odd feeling of both relief and disappointment.

How can I want to live for my kids on Earth and also wish for mercy and let me be free of my human lessons on Earth and see my sweet boy again at the same time? I don't know. I feel this paradox every day. I see the beauty in life, even in, and maybe especially in, the hardship. But sometimes, when I lose my higher perspective to the weight of the challenges it just feels like hell on Earth.

I told her I had lost my son. And she shared that they had recently lost their nephew. We hugged, multiple times. She knew there were no words to be exchanged outside of wishing me strength. I felt her compassion, not pity. She let me have the time and space needed to purge my grief fit, and I didn't feel like I had to hide it. Or apologize.

I am so grateful for these interactions. It truly is the kindness and compassion that sustains me. The connection and knowing that even in the presence of a kind stranger, I'm not alone. This knowing of how it feels to be on the receiving end of this kind of care ignites my passion even more to be that person for others. It doesn't take much—kind eyes, compassionate touch, holding space, and true empathy.

I love you.

February 22

I have noticed that the left side of my brain is capable of creating resource imaging of positive interactions with Noah while he was alive or connecting with Noah in positive ways in spirit. The right side of my brain pulls me into flashbacks and has a focus on the trauma of Noah's physical death. When I have a flashback, I catch it, if I can, and redirect my focus to the left side of my brain.

I had a realization the other day that just keeps getting reinforced through other conversations: I don't want the very small moment in time where Noah's body died to take over my relationship with him or be the majority of time my brain spends with him. I realized that I have the power (with PTSD treatment and the intention to do so) to move that memory into just a sliver in my brain, with the overwhelming "disc space" containing my wonderful memories of who Noah was on Earth and my current relationship with who he is in spirit. I want to honor him by focusing on who he was, not one decision or event. I want to focus on his life, not his physical death.

Tonight I went to an event honoring another sweet boy who died by suicide and our collective grief. His brave and brilliant mom shared a story reflecting his authentic, uninhibited, free, and fun spirit, and how his spirit serves as inspiration for us all to live authentically.

This made me reflect more, and I realized I'd like to spend time reflecting on and trying to embody who Noah was while in his physical body. Noah was brave, independent, strong, sensitive, funny, smart, creative, quiet, open-minded, silly, generous, thoughtful, caring, and as Hope reflected on tonight—even when he was being an independent teenager—he always made sure we knew that he loved us.

Being mindful and present with remembering Noah's essence and using it to inspire how I interact in the world is one way I can honor him.

I love you.

February 23

Our first professional pictures after Noah was born. I was holding him naked here and he peed all over my sweater. I was a younger mom—just twenty-six when Noah was born. I had no idea what I was doing as a parent of a newborn. I had no experience with babies, and we didn't have family support in Alaska, where we lived at the time.

I remember right after delivery, they took him and put him under a warmer, and when the doctor came in to check on us he asked why Noah was still there. We assumed someone was going to tell us what to do with him or the nurse would do something next. When we got home we had the wrong size diapers (he was a big newborn). He kept leaking, and we didn't realize it was because he needed a bigger size until someone told us. He was colicky, and I did not know how to soothe him outside of nursing. That always calmed him down, so that is where he stayed for many hours in the day and what he needed to sleep. I would try to roll away slowly to let him sleep, but the second my body was an inch away he would wake up and cry.

My sweet boy was so sensitive from his first breath to his last. He needed to feel loved, cared for, and close. He felt deeply. I think he just learned to hide it as he got older. In recent months, he told us that he would overthink things. Analyze situations over and over, trying to figure out if he had done something wrong. Kind of how I, and I think others that were close to Noah, have felt since his passing.

I found a book tonight that my dad had written inside of when I was a teenager, reflecting on our relationship. As I read each page, with his loving words, I was reminded about the simplicity of parenting in the face of all of the stressful and complex challenges we face: love.

My dad's messages in the book talked over and over about the importance of loving myself and his love for me. I think sometimes we overcomplicate things, and if we zoom out and just come at every interaction from a place of love and compassion, that's the best we can do. For ourselves and others. We're not going to be perfect, but with this intention, we'll get as close as humanly possible.

I love you.

February 24

I'm realizing that words I've heard, and even written myself, about how we "should" give ourselves love and compassion are somewhat hollow. Sounds great, but how do we go about doing that? I can tell myself something logically, but unless I go deep and figure out why I haven't been able to do that, process, figure out how to find that compassion, process, and then implement with consistency and intention, self-compassion is just a term that I know I "should" try to incorporate in my life.

It reminds me of when I got divorced. Everyone talked about "doing the work" to heal and find yourself. I had no idea what that meant. Could someone please give me some very detailed and specific guidance?

There are so many ways to go about "going deep" and I think we can use our inner wisdom to help guide us to what we need. Reading, researching, hearing stories of others, experiencing, listening to your gut, and then moving with intention and openness toward your own, very personal and unique healing journey. For someone who is a "thinker" and spends much of my time in my head, I do know that it likely doesn't rest in just the "understanding" or "knowing" of a wound or of the path to healing. It does require fully feeling, sensing, rewiring the brain, and processing in the mind, body, and soul. It's hard work. But I think it's the whole point of life.

I love you.

February 25

This trauma stuff is no joke. Our brains have taken a beating and recovery is long and slow.

How do we treat trauma? Many trauma-specific treatments focus on changing the brain's wiring to become more familiar with the parasympathetic response, rest/digest, rather than the sympathetic response, fight, flight, freeze. When we've experienced trauma, we live nearly all of our time in a highly activated (sympathetic) state with adrenaline and cortisol coursing through our veins.

Treatments range from electrodes training the brain, bilateral brain stimulation, tapping to engage the brain, meditation, breath work, etc. Our brain is truly an incredible organ. It can be shaped and manipulated in a negative way at the drop of a hat and can take months/years to recover.

At the crux of this is just providing the brain as many safe, positive experiences as possible and ingraining that into our neural pathways. The more time we spend in a safe space, having positive experiences, the easier it will be to find our way to calm when activated. Safety isn't a thought—it's a felt experience. The more you experience safety, the more your nervous system learns to trust and let its guard down.

At times I have felt very dissociated. And I've been encouraged to "ground." But grounding did not feel safe to me, being present in my life was not a place that brought me calm or ease. It has taken time to ease into the idea that I'm safe in the present moment. And much of that has come from realizing that I've survived eight months (today). And I've even experienced moments of joy, relaxation, and connection.

This positive time spent doesn't have to be through formal interventions (although they can certainly kick-start brain healing). It can be through co-regulation with another who can hold a calm and compassionate space, through safe touch, having more and more days go by where you haven't experienced a traumatic event, receiving the calming energy of nature, soaking or swimming in water, etc.

Noah Grants Hope.

I love you.

February 26

Today felt like the first day of spring. My first spring without Noah physically here. The school yearbook reached out about the spread they are doing for him. And the school year is coming to a close in a few short months.

I can't live in the "what would have beens" because that creates suffering, but I do notice his friends on the verge of being seniors. And it hurts my stomach and creates an awful lump in my throat.

I'm practicing letting these feelings hit me, feeling them, and then moving to a focus on the present moment. Feeling him now. I was in the backyard this morning with the sun shining through a light rain shower and I felt him with me.

I love you.

February 27

Please forgive me. I'm sorry. I love you. Thank you.[10]
May you be happy.
May you be peaceful.
May you be well.
May you live with ease.
May you find deep joy.
May you be free of pain.
May you be free from harm.
May you be free of suffering.
May I be happy.
May I be peaceful.
May I be well.
May I live with ease.
May I find deep joy.
May I be free of pain.
May I be free from harm.
May I be free of suffering.[11]
I love you.

---

10. Ho'oponopono

11. Adapted from Sharon Salzberg, *Lovingkindess Meditation: Learning to Love Through Insight Meditation (*Sounds True, 2005), audiobook.

February 28

Since the day Noah transitioned, I've prayed that I don't have to reincarnate again. I have felt like I don't have the strength to go through a life with challenges like this again. And then, the other day I had this overwhelming desire to have a "do over." I want the chance to be Noah's mom again, and this time I would do it better from the start, using all of the lessons I've learned as a guide.

There is so much wisdom that comes from experience. I would want to parent with a zoomed out perspective of what's important and not get caught up in what society tells me I should care about. I would want to have more patience and always operate from a place of love and not fear.

The human me wants a do over.

AND

I also know that I wouldn't know these things without making the mistakes that I have.

That's a shitty reality—knowing that you will hurt people you love or not respond in ways that are the most helpful. And that maybe we have to go through being on both the giving and receiving end of our imperfect humanness to evolve.

Unfortunately, perfectionism isn't real. And fortunately, we become better through all of our imperfect interactions.

I love you.

March 1

I spoke with Noah's prescribing doctor today. Something I have not been ready to do until just recently. One thing that he mentioned that really surprised me was that the majority of teens he sees come to him without their parents' knowledge and asking for medication to treat their depression or anxiety. In Oregon you can make your own, confidential medical decisions at age fourteen. This means that kids can consent to and take drugs that have a potential increased risk of suicide, especially within the first two week of beginning the medication, when dosage changes, when even one or two doses are missed, and that it's possible to overdose on them[12] … and there is no one there to monitor, discuss, help weigh the pros and cons, etc.

This means that the kids are relying solely on prescription meds to manage their mental health. When we know that not only does it not work for the majority of kids, but even for those it does, it does not address the root cause of their suffering.

This seems to be a huge flaw in the system. I believe (my educated guess) a system that was originally created to allow kids access to birth control, abortion, and related medication, not mental health care.

Parents: Please talk to your kids. If it seems like they are depressed or struggling, open the lines of communication so they can feel comfortable coming to you, so that you can be as in the loop and present as possible. Our kids need help figuring this out—how to address the root causes, and access to and knowledge of other interventions that don't carry the same risk and side effects as antidepressants.

I love you.

---

12. Stephen P. Cuffe and William S. Hall, "Do Antidepressants Increase the Risk of Suicide in Children and Adolescents?" American Academy of Children & Adolescent Psychiatry, accessed March 2025, https://www.aacap.org/aacap/medical_students_and_residents/mentorship_matters/developmentor/Do_Antidepressants_Increase_the_Risk_of_Suicide_in_Children_and_Adolescents.aspx.

March 2

Nothing real is ever lost.

"Approaching death and death itself, the dissolution of the physical form, is always a great opportunity for spiritual realization. This opportunity is tragically missed most of the time, since we live in a culture that is almost totally ignorant of death, as it is almost totally ignorant of anything that truly matters.

Every portal (to awakening) is a portal of death, the death of the false self. When you go through it, you cease to derive your identity from your psychological, mind-made form. You then realize that death is an illusion, just as your identification with form was an illusion. The end of illusion- that's all that death is. It is painful only as long as you cling to illusion." —Eckhart Tolle, The Power of Now, *p. 119*

March 3

I've explored the concept of duality quite a bit since Noah's transition. It was so clear to me that love and pain are almost the same thing, two sides of a very thin coin. This is also true for happiness, pleasure, etc. Another life-changing gem from Eckhart Tolle:

"The Buddha taught that even your happiness is dukkha—a Pali word meaning suffering or unsatisfactoriness. It is inseparable from the opposite. This means that your happiness and unhappiness are in fact one. Only the illusion of time separates them." —Eckhart Tolle, The Power of Now, *p. 154*

Because nothing outside of ourselves stays the same, eventually happiness will become unhappiness and on and on. Once we realize that everything passes away, we no longer fear loss. He goes on to say that this isn't being negative, but rather it just prevents us from pursuing an illusion for the rest of our lives.

While things or people can bring temporary pleasure, happiness, etc. nothing can give you joy. Joy is found within as a product of "being." Being is a state of acceptance, peace, ease, flow, and presence in the NOW.

A Course in Miracles says: "No one who is at one with himself can even conceive of conflict."[13]

I told Grant yesterday, half joking, that when I get to a point where nothing has a lasting effect on me and I'm not emotionally reactive, then I know I've reached enlightenment. I was half joking because it sounds nearly impossible, but I have this feeling in my body that I can get close.

If I can make the progress I've made in working toward acceptance of Noah's transition, I can do anything. This is the

---

13. Helen Schucman, "Lesson 340," *A Course in Miracles* (Foundation for Inner Peace, 1976).

work I find most important. I'm so grateful to Noah for this shift in my awareness.

Tolle quotes *A Course in Miracles*: "Most people need to experience a great deal of suffering before they will relinquish resistance and accept" (p. 127). This is the concept of Post Traumatic Growth that academics (including me!) are now studying. We've known it as a concept in spiritual study for ages, but I'm curious to know how we might maximize this massive opportunity to better humanity.

I love you.

March 4

I had an image pop into my head the other day of the Mario Brothers video game. I imagined jumping and leaping to get all of the coins as how we might see our role in life's challenges.

What if we saw life's next challenge as the coin we actually want to get? We see its value in our ability to get through the next challenge. We enthusiastically leap toward it and take it for all its worth.

We don't label it as bad. It's neutral and just a part of life. We see and understand its bigger role and purpose. We know and accept that there will be challenge after challenge. That's what the game of life is. And so we take each coin that is presented to us as the gift that it is for our spiritual growth.

But we have to choose to not only play, but to play enthusiastically and with the calm knowing that with each challenge, the process is helping us to find and rescue the Princess (i.e., our higher selves).

I love you.

March 5

I've been thinking a lot about my perspective on the importance of doing this deep inner work in contrast to taking a pill to get us through. I'm going back and forth in my logical mind, wondering if that can actually make a difference for folks with really significant mental health challenges. I don't want to be advocating for something that isn't actually helpful. I think that in and of itself can be detrimental—being told that if you do the work, you can be better. And maybe you don't know how to do the work, you don't have the resources ... it's not accessible in one way or the other. Shame, shoulds, or expectations aren't helpful.

Maybe it's not a question of doing the deep work *or* taking a pill. Maybe it's neither.

This led to my next thought: Why are we trying to "fix" and pathologize so much? I have definitely seen things in my children that worried me and made me think I needed to figure out how to change whatever it was that worried me. I see something that isn't optimal, and I'm in fixer mode.

Maybe not all challenges are bad. Maybe we just need to sit with others in a loving and compassionate presence without giving the impression that the person needs to be fixed. I've seen this in my own personal journey through grief. Nobody can fix it for me. I don't want to feel like I need to be fixed. I want to feel my feelings, have them honored and normalized, and know that I have resources to access when I'm ready.

I think the difference in approach is "fix" versus "guide." We can offer possible resources or guidance, but not in order to fix someone but rather to love and support them in their perfect wholeness as they are right now.

I wish I had done more of that for Noah. I am actively reminding myself of this for all of the years left that I have with Grant and Hope and other loved ones.

I love you.

March 6

We often strive to manifest positive things in our lives. But how do we truly know what is positive or negative?

"Do you have the bigger picture? There have been many people for whom limitation, failure, loss, illness, or pain in whatever form turned out to be their greatest teacher. It taught them to let go of false self-image and superficial ego-dictated goals and desires. It gave them depth, humility, and compassion. It made them more real." —*Eckhart Tolle,* The Power of Now, *p. 177*

So, when we talk about wanting a specific outcome in life, how do we know what's best for our higher good? I've realized that instead of thinking I know what's best for me, I surrender to what life presents me. And I am choosing to see the beauty and great gift in all things, what we humanly perceive as both positive and negative.

This shift in perspective is the key to finding peace. It removes the fear and suffering, and allows us to consciously grow through each event or condition we experience.

I still struggle to implement this "knowing" in my life. But I am beginning to notice when I see something as good or bad, and I consciously remind myself to zoom out and try to see everything from a higher perspective. Practice makes, not perfect, but progress.

I love you.

March 7

Resistance. Suffering. Surrender.

It has become clear that the path to awakening is often through suffering. But it's not the suffering that creates the awakening—it's the surrender.

Sometimes it takes an extraordinary pain to force us to yield to the reality of a situation that cannot be changed. In my case, it has felt like my only choice. If I toiled in resistance, I would be living every second in my own unique hell.

On the way to and even in the midst of my path to surrender, I have had to be brave enough to feel it all. To fully feel my intense and deep pain and love. And in doing so, I have been present with it. My presence has in and of itself been my surrender.

This has felt like an involuntary reaction. My body and heart haven't seen another way. I am still in the process of fully surrendering. Not just to Noah's transition but as a way of being in life in general.

The part I struggle with, that doesn't feel automatic, is quieting my mind. It seems to butt in occasionally, telling me a story about the past. And when we give power to the past, forgiveness is hard. When I notice this happening, I remind myself that the only thing that is real, is the now. Right now, Noah's spirit and essence are alive and with me. Right now, I am awake and conscious. Right now, I feel immense love and compassion. Right now, I am peacefully surrendered.

Surrender doesn't mean giving up. In Tolle's words, it's yielding to, rather than opposing the flow of life. We can still take action and have intention. But like water in a river with the intention of flowing to the ocean, we bob and weave around obstacles with ease. If a boulder is in the way, we flow around and maybe take a detour or another path. Water doesn't push up against the boulder and try to will it to move; it doesn't become angry, upset that the boulder is there, it doesn't give up and turn around. Resistance has no power, and only hurts us.

Feel. Flow. Ease. Peace.

This is what I'm practicing.

I love you.

March 8

I've found Noah. I've been looking for him everywhere—the clouds, in nature, synchronicities, messages from others—but I don't have to make him try so hard anymore to connect with me.

In my Helping Parents Heal group, they say our children are as close as our next breath. But I've found him even closer. I didn't notice at first, but I've found him inside of me. What a gift to know without a shadow of a doubt that he is not just near when I ask him to be, but he is literally a part of me. There, with me, on a soul level, everywhere I go.

We are always one with those we love.

Thank God I found him.

I love you.

March 9

I've been thinking a lot about labels and the power of words.

Depressed. Anxious. Mentally ill. Bereaved. Died. Gone. Lost. Grief. Suicide. Chronic.

They all sound so hopeless. And what is the point of labeling someone as hopeless? What would happen if instead of labeling ourselves or someone else, we refrained from thinking about, identifying with, or creating stories about an experience? What if we just noticed the experience? When we label ourselves we cement the stories we've made up about our experiences in our heads, we reinforce hopelessness.

Labels create resistance ... I don't want to be depressed, anxious, bereaved, mentally ill, etc.

We all have challenging emotions, experiences, and conditions. But, in my opinion labeling them is detrimental. It separates us from each other instead of unifying us as humans, having normal responses to the human condition.

What if, instead, we feel fully. Stay present with our experiences, emotions, and current capacity. With the knowing that it's possible they will change at any moment. What if the attention we paid to them in the present actually brings light to them? Giving them full attention is surrender. And surrender allows for movement and change. An opportunity for a new emotion, condition, or response. We are never one thing. And nothing stays the same. We know these things as universal truths.

I am committed to seeing someone for who they are as a whole—not just in a moment. To being present. And to using language that promotes hope, change, and connection.

Month
9

March 10

One of the things Noah struggled with was self-compassion. To be soft with himself. And this is the thing I struggle with the most.

I'm just realizing I don't have to master figuring out how to live after this massive shift in my reality. I don't have to figure out what my contribution to the world is going to be. I don't have to keep busy.

I just need to be. In the present moment. To be soft with myself. And know that that's good enough. That I have the same worth as if I was saving the world.

My intentions for myself right now are to find peace, to figure out how to find joy again, and to be present with myself and my loved ones.

In my eyes, that is more than enough for my kids. That has to be enough for me, too.

March 11

When a tree falls with no one around to hear it, does it make a sound?

When a heart loves, and there is no other being around to receive it, does it still love?

I had a realization today that perhaps one of the reasons losing a physical presence to love is so painful is because it feels like we have lost the ability to even feel the love that was meant for that person at all. And, at least for me, there is a fear that if I lost everyone close to me, would I even continue to exist? Would the feeling of love just disappear?

But do we not continue to have unlimited love emanating from our hearts? Are we not all made up of love as our essence? And can that love not also be directed toward ourselves? Knowing that we are one with all that has been created. Our love can flow effortlessly to our individual human selves, knowing that we are not individual or separate at all and that we are all made up of one energy.

Deep Tuesday night thoughts from Grant's music rehearsal parking lot.

I love you.

March 12

At the beginning of the year, I set an intention to be as present as possible. To be here now. I see how much this one principle can shift our realities and reduce suffering.

As life seems to be accelerating and trying to return to a "normal" chaotic pace, I am reminding myself of the most important things to me—taking time to connect with myself, with community, and with Noah and my spirit family.

It takes a conscious awareness of time and presence to prioritize and protect these things. Zooming out and remembering that so many of the things we think matter, that keep us stressed and busy, really don't matter. We can give ourselves so much more grace than we do.

Try to remember and actively prioritize what is most important to you.

I love you.

March 13

I don't know why it's just hitting me, but on my school drop-off drive this morning, I finally saw so clearly the relationship between loving yourself and creating your own reality. It's something that spiritual teachers speak of frequently, but it hit differently in my heart today.

What we give to others, the planet, animals, etc. will supposedly manifest and flow back to us. So, if we are full of chaos, anger, despair, feel a sense of lack, etc, we cannot truly give much else. We can only give what we have. So, it follows that we must find peace, abundance, love, etc. in ourselves first. That is the first step. Once we have that, it will radiate out into the world effortlessly and be reflected back to us in our interactions with the world.

This is no simple task, especially when we are not zoomed out. One could very well ask how I could not be full of despair after my son transitioned by suicide. Or how they can be full of love and gratitude in the midst of something we see as awful. First, we must feel all of it. But it is possible to feel all of it and also be grateful and full of love at the same time. To see the beauty in the mess. To feel the full range of emotion is possible. I know because I'm in it.

When we zoom out, we can pull ourselves out of the doom, stress, or even out of the transient things that bring us happiness or distraction in the moment. We can more easily see the greater purpose of our existence and our own personal expression of love as souls having a human experience.

This is my simple human mind path:

1. ZOOM OUT.
2. Know your true self as love.
3. Use that knowing as a lens to create and view your own internal reality.
4. Effortlessly radiate that loving knowing into the world.
5. Be surrounded by this loving goodness that emanates from you and is reflected back in all of your interactions.

I love you.

March 14

I'm observing the differences in how people approach grief and trauma. And the various types of help I've been drawn to at different times. All of them can be helpful, and seem to build upon another. Kind of like Maslow's hierarchy of needs. But this is a hierarchy of transformation.

I'm realizing we must resource ourselves first before doing the really deep work if we haven't already done it before our most recent lifequake. Resourcing can look like basic self-care, nervous system regulation, tools to manage dissociation, panic, sleep, etc. This is essential and nothing can really be done until this has been addressed.

Next, we need normalization of what we've experienced to know we're not alone. We need our deep emotion to be witnessed in community.

Next is intellectual understanding. We want to understand the deeper purpose of what we've been through, of life, or existence. Why did this happen? What are the practical things that caused it or contributed to it? Is there science to back up what we're experiencing mentally, emotionally, physically?

Once we have the facts down, we turn to spiritual exploration. This is when we do research, have conversations, read, write, attend rituals, services, healing circles, etc. These tools become important for our existential inquiry. Even if we had previously held beliefs, we question everything. We have been stripped down to nothing and are building a new foundation.

We soon realize that while we make progress in our heads we must turn to our hearts and bodies to understand what they are holding onto, and we work to find somatic release. We begin the work to understand the intersection of what our bodies know, what our minds know, and what our deeper inner spiritual knowing is.

But we can't stop here. We have done the deep inner work, and now we release the need for outside influence, healing, etc.

We know that we have everything inside of us that we will ever need to find peace, joy, and unconditional love, no matter the outside circumstances.

Each step feels like a major victory. But we should hold onto the knowledge that there is always more to be explored and held.

I love you.

March 15

What an absolute gift to be a vessel to bring my children's souls into material form.

Such a powerful paradigm shift to see them as their own, unique, powerful souls on their own journeys rather than "my children."

I have really felt the beautiful weight and depth of being a mother as of late. Reliving the miracle of growing a human with a soul inside of my womb. The insane act of childbirth, and the tremendous love it takes to tend to these helpless little beings day in and day out, for so long.

What an honor to be such a significant part of another soul's incarnation and learning. It is such a blessing to be a part of such a beautiful mess—the mess of learning, making mistakes, and growing together with our children.

Such a beautiful fucking mess. And I'm grateful for it all.

Thank you. Thank you. Thank you.

I love you.

March 16

As I come across other people who are experiencing lifequakes, I've thought to myself that I should know exactly what to say or do because I've been through something so incredibly challenging, and I'm finding my way through it. I've felt like I should have something helpful to offer.

This morning, as we got news of a neighbor's terminal diagnosis via text we saw so many comments in the text thread … from "life's not fair," "screw 2025," "this is devastating"to "we're here to help in any way we can," "we love you," etc.

I had a reaction to the negative comments because I know for me, hearing things like that has not been helpful. As I reflected, I realized that none of us really know what is helpful. And we don't know what someone else is feeling or needs to hear.

I realized that everyone processes challenges differently and goes through various stages and phases of processing. I don't think there is one right way to approach someone going through the shit. We can't assume anything. Especially as it's often a time of huge shifts in paradigms, spirituality, priorities, etc.

The only approach that seems appropriate—no matter someone's take on life, death, life after death—is to offer love and support. No advice. No education. No attempted solutions.

Just loving presence. Emanate love. In the now.

I love you.

March 17

This time last year, I took my kids and their friends to Costa del Sol, Spain.

This time last year. You never know what life is going to bring. The only thing we know is that things will change. I'm so grateful we took this trip.

I took Noah to Thailand the year prior and still wanted him to experience Europe before he entered his last high school years. I've always wanted my kids to see at least part of the world so they would be inspired to continue exploring it on their own once they left the nest.

I had envisioned Noah taking a gap year or two, Grant going with him for the second year. Hoping he could convince his best friend to join for at least a few months.

Now the future looks different. We are so naive when we make far-off future plans. You'd think after forty-three years on Earth, I'd know better.

I'm beginning to see the power and beauty in surrendering to the flow of life. That I can set a broad intention of seeing and being open to following the opportunities that life presents, which feel full of love, peace, and joy. To honor when things feel forced or out of alignment and to change whatever circumstances are available to change when I can. And when they can't, like Noah's physical presence being gone, to go with the flow. Accept. Move with the energy that is real and palpable. That flow has led me down a beautiful path, one where I get to deepen my relationship with not only Noah, but with my other spirit family, my physical family and loved ones, and my own soul.

Wow. What a gift to go with the flow instead of toil in resistance. I can't imagine my life any other way.

Thank you, Noah, for this beautiful gift of perspective. You are amazing and I am so lucky to have been your mom and to continue to be so connected with you.

I love you all.

March 18

What is luck?

I'm solidifying my belief that luck is not actually a "thing."

In the past, when I would say I was lucky to have an opportunity or experience, I was often reminded that I had worked hard and my "luck" was a combination of that hard work and opportunity.

Today, I think that "luck" is just the universe aligning for your highest good. Not because you have worked so hard, but because you have surrendered to moving with what the energy is trying to tell you.

I've been listening to a book on harnessing the flow of universal energy. How if something feels like a burden, like it's hard work, or somehow forced then it is not for us. We need to stop forcing a square peg into a round hole and instead flow to the opening that receives us with ease.

I've thought about this in relation to careers, school, relationships, and even our passions. Our society loves to make us feel like we need to work hard to be in a certain place to be successful. What if your work, relationships, and personal goals felt easy?

When we flow with our higher purpose, life will put up roadblocks for those things not meant for us. The roadblocks aren't for us to figure out how to knock them down. They are there to divert us to the next opportunity. Nothing should feel like a choice we have to perseverate on—it should feel so obvious, easy, and aligned that there is no choice at all.

Roadblocks, failures, missed opportunities ... these are all deemed negative because of our perception. What if we changed our perception to see them as positive and helpful communications from the universe—guide posts telling us this isn't the way? Relax, stop fighting and resisting, and see what is offered to you.

Since Noah transitioned, I have been wondering what my path is. And I've been reminded that my path is exactly where I am. And the next step on my path will be presented to me as it serves me. I don't need to "figure it out" or work to make something happen.

I hope to not be lucky; but rather, to be aligned and flow with the unexpected and beautiful places, people, and experiences that are meant for me.

March 19

Noah and I went to the grocery store shortly after his second birthday, and he pointed to a cake in the bakery. He said he wanted to turn two, meaning he wanted the cake with candles and singing again. So, of course we got the cake and "turned two" again.

As I've mentioned probably more than once, I've prayed that I would never have to reincarnate again. That my soul is tired, and I don't feel like I could make it. But as I'm moving along on my journey, I realize that the goal is to find heaven on Earth no matter what my circumstances are. To find that internal sense of being part of the universe and to feel the joy of that. To maintain my internal peace even if it seems to be chaos outside of me. When I can do this, I not only am able to be on Earth as long as my destiny says I should be, but I can be here, now, feeling peace, joy, and love. This seems so simple, it's so powerful, and is our biggest challenge as humans. It feels like a light has been switched on in me ... like I can finally see this truth and the path. It's fun and exciting to be able to practice this as challenges arise, as they always will.

I see that my ability to do this impacts those around me in a really positive way, the ripple effect.

To live consciously and in a way where I can live from my internal peace and joy is a practice. It's an awareness of when I am feeling disregulated, overwhelmed, or like I don't know how I'm surviving, that I can then purposefully shift to feel my internal sense of being.

A big part of my ability to do this is to see physical death and struggle differently. To shift my perspective out of fear to understanding and seeing the bigger picture. This is a critical piece for how I am now living my life.

Living unconsciously keeps me in seeing what's just in front of me instead of zooming out.

Perspective is everything.

March 20

Since Noah transitioned, I've become fascinated with near-death experiences (NDE). When I'm having a day where I need a little boost or reminder of what my reality actually is versus what most of society see as my reality, I watch a recounting of an NDE. I'm in awe listening to these stories as folks who come back from dying have very similar accounts of what happened, and almost always feel changed to their core by the experience. To me, there is no denying the validity and power of their experiences.

A common thing noted in these experiences is the feeling of not wanting to return to their body, to their human life, and relishing in the unexplainable feeling of immense unconditional love.

The part that seemed incomprehensible to me is that many speak about seeing their loved ones crying, grief-stricken, suffering … and yet they still don't want to come back.

But now, I think I realize why. It's because they are finally zoomed out all of the way, to see that all is good no matter what. All is in divine order. That we create our own suffering, and we could just get out of our own way if we could become fully conscious and change our perspective. That we are learning valuable lessons from our challenges.

They have immense compassion and love for us. But they are not worried, and they know we are okay, even if we don't feel that way.

I love you.

March 21

I've been taking the time to notice my body and how it impacts my ability to feel connected to Noah. When I am feeling tense it is largely because of fear-based thoughts that lead to anxiety. And when I'm tense, it's impossible for me to feel my deep connection with Noah—the one where I can feel his signature energy coursing through my body. The one that is most significant to me, that I feel so intensely and instantly brings a smile to my face and peace to my heart.

To really feel Noah inside of me, I need to be soft. To feel peace and calm. To be in a state of acceptance and knowing instead of rigid resistance and fear. To be in the present moment, conscious, aware, open, and connected.

The second piece that I have come to know is that before I had learned to connect with my own soul- that is, when I run around doing my Earthly human tasks and am not living consciously, in the present moment, I miss connecting with my own soul. I am just along for the wild human ride without a deeper sense of purpose and with a lot of unnecessary suffering.

It makes sense that if we can't deeply connect with our own souls, we can't deeply connect with our ascended loved ones. It is essential for me to truly know in my being that we are all connected energetically and we are so much more than our human bodies.

I believe this is why those who have had significant people in their lives transition often become motivated to understand who they are at their core. They understand on some level that their ability to maintain their connection with their loved one is dependent on their ability to see and know themselves.

What a gift this illusion of death gives us if we are willing to receive it.

I love you.

March 22

Today, I'm in the mess of grief. I am feeling my human experience emotions of missing my boy in his human form. His personality. His body. His hugs. His smile. His curls. His slender fingers and toes. His twinkle eyes. His playfulness. His humor. His mischievousness. His bravery. His generosity. His genuine, kind nature.

I will never experience those things again. He is in his spirit form. And I have a feeling that when I become my spirit form too, I won't care about or miss all of the human things.

I understand that identification with the body or personality is ego. That at our core, what lives eternally is our essence. And at the same time I'm an evolving soul having a human experience. And my human self, that has not shed all of my ego, misses these human things.

Right now, I ache for the only version of him I've known since I gave birth to him. I am letting myself feel it all. Giving in to the heartbreak so that it can continue to soften over time.

March 23

"Dying is absolutely safe" —*Ram Dass*

I meditated on a picture of a beautiful flowering tree this morning. Nature perfectly mimics and offers guidance for our human existence.

The flowers were birthed slowly over time, shined bright through their life and gracefully fell to the garden floor, waiting to be returned to the Earth.

The flower doesn't cling to the branch, afraid to fall. The other flowers don't resist and do everything they can to keep all of that season's flowers on the tree.

They know there is only one way in the cycle. And there is no changing the cycle. We move from one moment to the next and accept each new reality given to us in those moments.

Each is beautiful if we can just stop clinging and creating a story that the only real life is that where we are firmly attached to material form.

I love you.

March 24

Noah was known for his smirk ... this smirk and his big toothy, beautiful smile are my favorite ways to see him in my imagination.

I've been thinking about love and relationships a lot lately. What is true love? What purpose do relationships have in our lives? How do we let our love and light shine without barriers or shadows? How would doing that impact our relationships?

In the moment, when the kids were little, I of course loved them with all of my heart, and at the same time, I had so much going on in my life that I now see maybe prevented all of that love from flowing out of my heart and into theirs. I felt my love for them fully in my heart, but I had layers of shame, grief, unmet expectations, the inability to fully receive, and perfectionism ... these layers created the barrier to allowing the love that was inside of me from fully flowing.

I did not see my barriers. I didn't even know they existed; they were just a part of me. These parts that I was not acknowledging. I was unconsciously living, trying my best, but not fully seeing myself. The true me—not the layers of baggage I had accumulated.

Our kids, of course, have no clue about our layers, our barriers. They are just along for the ride of being our children. They are impacted by our barriers, but don't quite understand why we react or behave the way we do.

It's my intention to uncover all of my hidden parts that cast shadows on my true self. I want my kids to understand this human condition that we all have in common. And to ultimately feel and know my true, uncovered, and bright love. Without the barriers. And in doing so, I will know it myself.

Thank you, Noah, for this gift of insight and wisdom. Thank you for your forgiveness. Thank you for your unconditional love and acceptance.

I love you.

March 25

This body that I grew in my belly. That I birthed. That I cared for. I love this body.

It playfully adventured. It ran. It snuggled. It swam and dove. It hacky sacked. It skateboarded. It relaxed. It did flips and handstands.

And at the very same time I find there are times where I have contempt for this body. I hate the spinal condition that led to chronic pain. I despise the genetics that led to mental health challenges.

Also at the very same time, I appreciate everything that made human Noah, Noah. He was the Noah we knew and loved, I'm sure, in part, because of these struggles. How is it possible to love and despise something at the same time? To see the pain and beauty created in the same organism?

This duality exists in everything. This purpose behind the struggle. The yin and the yang. The reason for suffering and the reason for the expansion.

I see it all. Someday I'll see it without the labels of good or bad and just see it as it is. Everything and nothing at the same time.

March 26

Noah knew how to be playful. To be light. To be adventurous. To be brave. To be authentic. To be funny. To be silly.

He joined sibling dance parties, dressed up with his sister, made funny faces, played practical jokes, made up stories to get a reaction … his essence was playful and at the same time solid and genuine.

I'm lucky enough to get to feel his essence in my body. And I know these are qualities that I want to strengthen and cultivate in myself.

I am allowing myself to channel my inner Noah.

Thank you, buddy.

I love you.

March 27

A Buddhist monk I recently met said that the reason it's important to meditate everyday is because we need to consistently make time to face ourselves.

This is living consciously and awake.

When we face ourselves we get to feel and acknowledge our core essence of love and see where we could cultivate that more. We begin to trust ourselves and our role in the universe, thus reducing fear and anxiety. We see where we are resisting and where we can loosen the grip to create a better flow. We observe our human selves and have compassion.

The monk shared that anything we do that gets rid of the insane chatter in our heads allows us time with ourselves. This is what I've started to call "the flow." Maybe it's through art, exercise, movement, relaxation, breath work, reading, music, creation ... it doesn't matter, as long as you're focused and your monkey mind is quiet.

This is the most important thing in life. To face and truly know oneself.

Five minutes a day is all it takes. And then you'll start to get addicted to the feeling and will want to be in this quiet flow state more and more.

I love you.

March 28

Love these boat ragamuffins. We lived simply and ruggedly on the boat, with a few pieces of clothing, mostly barefoot, and with no functioning mirror. The picture doesn't do it justice, but I remember this moon looking like it was taking up the entire horizon ... the magic of being human and playing on Mother Earth.

When Noah transitioned, I was beside myself. Literally leaving painful marks on my head as I tried to pull what my eyes had seen and my brain was trying to process out of my head. I couldn't mentally or physically handle what I was going through. I wondered how I was supposed to live like this.

I was eventually able to dissociate enough to function for the most part—this is how the body protects the mind and soul.

I believe I'm still using that tool, but now am dipping my toe into different realities that have felt impossible to let my heart fully process. I am only able to do that because through my calmer, dissociated state, I have been able to do some Soul Work, to understand the spiritual truth behind life and death.

I dip my toe in until I intuitively know I've reached my limit. Then, I come back to my knowing and resourcing for as long as I need to regulate and feel safe enough to dip my toe in a little bit more.

I wish I didn't have to dip into the harsh reality of my new life. But I know that if I don't process what my human form has been through, it will stay there in the background and rear its ugly head at some point.

If I'm doing neither—dipping my toe in nor staying present in my spiritual resourcing—that is when I'm living unconsciously. Living this way eventually leads to the ugly head rearing—flashbacks, panic, denial, and disbelief.

I've found it has to be a very intentional back and forth. All while trying to live life and do all of the "normal" things we have to do to function in society and in relationships.

This is my full-time job. It is survival. And at the same time it is a great awakening. It takes time and consistent focus and effort. It's fucking hard. The hardest thing I've ever done. I'm tired. But I can't give up. I see the light at the end of the tunnel and more and more even in "the now."

March 29

The last several days as I was deeply missing my boy in physical form, I asked him to help me. And as he does pretty reliably, he showed up. Often he has to wait for me to be asleep because when I'm awake my mind is in a state that creates barriers to receiving him. He came to me in a dream ... he was his teenage self with no shirt on. Casually walking toward me, returning from some adventure. I got to hug him. Feel his skin. His hair. His warmth. His love. He smiled. I could feel him telling me this was his response to my request.

I've also recently reconnected with my dad. I really had forgotten that I could talk to him and ask for his help and guidance. When I was living unconsciously, I was just busy going about my human tasks. It's so easy to forget. But I'm back on the frequency of connection.

I love this frequency. It's intoxicating. Connection with our true nature as love and our oneness with our loved ones is everything. This is real life. Everything else is our imagination.

March 30

My mind continues to go in circles, wondering what I could have done better or differently in the past as a parent. How I could have better supported and guided my kids. How can I be better now and in the future for my kids? I laughed to myself during my meditation this morning as I was doing it again. I do this often and I always come back to the same thing, using various forms of the same logic to get there. I don't know why I think I'll find another answer that somehow gives me a new perspective. At this point, after many hundreds of hours of contemplating, I feel pretty solidly that it's all about loving ourselves.

I can reflect back on all of the times I failed to be the best version of myself for the kids, and if I dig just a little bit into what triggered me in those moments, it was a lack of compassion and love for myself and a fear that I didn't know what I was doing. That I didn't know how to control my kids into being perfect little humans with perfect lives who wouldn't have the same issues I did. Which is, of course, a paradox.

The attempt at control, wanting to make everything perfect—while an act seemingly from love—actually hurts. We don't want our kids to have to deal with the harsh consequences from their actions, and so we try to control variables that might lead to hardship. Partially for them, and partially for ourselves. Because it hurts to see your kids struggle. Our reactions to our children's issues are based on our own unresolved issues, and without fail, our lack of compassion for ourselves in dealing with those issues.

Relationships are mirrors. They are our greatest teachers. But only if we're willing to examine why we respond to situations the way we do. Only then can we be our best selves for our children.

I love you.

March 31

Just after I wrote my post yesterday, I read a chapter in *A New Earth* that spoke to much of what I was contemplating. Tolle expanded on my thoughts and talked about how we identify with roles we play in life (wife, mother, worker, etc), but none of those roles is our true selves.

Our true selves can't be found by "doing" anything in a certain role, but rather by being.

He spoke to the deep longing that children have to be "seen" by their parent, to have their parent there as a fellow human being, not as a role.

"Doing is never enough if you neglect being." (p. 103)

Being is looking, listening, touching, or helping. Being present, not wanting anything other than that moment as it is. This allows the child to be seen as a fellow being, and not just on the level of material form.

It's easy to get caught in the "doing" part of caregiving: Did you eat, bathe, do your school work, etc.? We lose sight of what life and relationships are all about: humans "being" together.

I've made a concerted effort over the years to tell my kids I'm sorry when I've not been my best self or when I've caught myself or they've caught me being too focused on the "doing." But this take on it gives this a new depth for me to notice. Nothing that needs to be done is really so important that we neglect really being with the souls we birthed into human form.

In Noah's words: Be chill. I think we can all use a little more of that energy.

April 1

"The paradox is that suffering is caused by identification with form and erodes identification with form. A lot of it is caused by the ego, although eventually suffering destroys the ego—but not until you suffer consciously." —Eckhart Tolle, A New Earth, *p. 12*

The "ego" is said to be all of the parts of ourselves that we identify with but are just things our mind has made up. It's not who we are at our core. It's everything that obscures our true essence, our "being," our "light."

I've said that my suffering has felt like the ground has been abruptly taken out from underneath me. I have been leveled. It has forced me into the present moment, as nothing else seems to exist outside of my current existence. Nothing makes sense, and I must rebuild my sense of who I am.

This is the removal of the ego through suffering. It can last for a moment, hours, days, or a lifetime. It all depends on whether you choose to continue consciously observing your circumstances, your emotions, etc. as the observer of life, or if you choose to identify with your circumstances and emotions, giving them power to consume and define you.

I find my suffering comes in waves. It intensifies when I identify with my human body and mind as my true reality, with my role as a bereaved mother, with materialism. It softens and begins to transmute into light when I feel free of these ego identifications and feel my true essence, and most of all, when I feel in my soul that we are all eternally connected.

There are a few practical things that help me find that place of peaceful presence—meditation, spending time with and chatting with like-minded people, reading books that are full of reminders, plant medicine, quiet alone time to face my true self, Internal Family Systems (IFS) therapy, and communing with nature.

And the constant reminder to "be chill." A soft and accepting intention to find more and more moments of this peace without the feeling of "needing" or grasping for it.

Flow. Allowance for all parts of me to show up. Gentle intention. Grace. Compassion. Love.

I believe if we can help our children to know this path, we can effectively alleviate much of the mental health crisis we find our kids in.

April 2

We are not alone in our suffering. I am noticing how significant it is for me to be witnessed in my sorrow. For these parts of life to be seen for what they are—universal.

I do not wish suffering on anyone else; however, the communities I am a part of, where we share and understand a common loss are of tremendous value to me. Normalizing death, loss, suicide, child death by any means, and then normalizing learning to live again after these experiences, is a major part of my healing.

Knowing that I am not the only person who has felt like it's a very tall order to continue living after a child loss ...

Knowing that I am not alone in feeling as if truly feeling the depth of emotion related to this loss might actually kill me ...

Knowing that I am not the only person working to find meaning in the darkness ...

Knowing that we all feel intense lows and intense highs throughout our human experience ...

Knowing that another's heart can feel my heart and I can fully feel another's heart ...

Knowing that our collective energy is one and we are never alone. We can be real with each other.

I am here with you. And I feel you here with me.

I love you.

April 3

I used to not be able to understand how relationships or love could include the concept of non-attachment. How could you not be attached to those you love? How can you not be devastated by losing them, either by way of break-up, divorce, a move, deployment, or death?

As I sit with this feeling of missing my boy, I'm contemplating what attachment is. I feel several things ...

I deeply miss his physically and emotionally connected presence in my life.

I feel his pain, which wasn't mine, and that I couldn't control, in my own body.

I wish I could have seen the man he was going to grow into. I was just starting to see him look more and more like a man.

I think about what it was like to be pregnant. I couldn't see him and his growth with my eyes. I couldn't have a conversation with him. I couldn't take away his discomfort. But I could feel him inside of me. I could feel our bond, our love, and that we were one, connected always.

I used to tease Noah that I wished the cord had never been cut. That I just wanted him back in my belly so I could keep him safe, always. I was only half joking—I really felt that, but of course I knew that it sounded crazy. Now I think it doesn't sound so crazy, but instead of wanting it to keep him safe, I know I have desired that feeling because it is actually our true nature to feel that connected, to feel that we truly are one.

Missing someone's individual and unique human, physical aspects is normal. And at the same time I realize that it is very much living in the past or the imaginary future. Maybe it's possible to turn the "missing" of the past into gratitude for the beautiful experience of being his human mom. And the "missing" of the imaginary future into a realization that it never existed to begin with and to focus on the present, where the only true reality exists.

When I'm in the present, I feel him inside of me. Just like I did when I was physically growing him inside of me. I feel his essence, his presence, his love, and our eternal connectedness.

I love you.

April 4

There are no words.

I know this and everyone who has wanted to support our family knows this.

That is why talk therapy can only do so much when processing grief and trauma.

Emotions are expressed through the body. So much is only felt in the body. And can only be processed through the body.

It's scary to physically feel this deep suffering. It seems likely it will actually kill you to feel it all. It has not been possible for me to open that door without the help of plant medicine.

I honestly don't know how I would have been able to face and process my trauma without the help of plant medicine. Traditional therapies couldn't touch my wound. Even EMDR, which is the gold standard for trauma, has been too much for my system. And while it helps with trauma, it does not facilitate the deep spiritual work to process the grief.

I've only scratched the surface of this processing. My system only allows bits and pieces as I'm ready. But with the help of plant medicine and my integration guide and therapy, I feel hopeful that I will find a way to not just survive but thrive and find my way to helping others.

I have been hesitant to share this part of my journey, but I think it's my duty to share what is actually helping me to alchemize this pain. I'm not doing it alone. I have an amazing guide that is helping me to prepare for my journeys and to integrate the gems that come from them. I have had massive somatic releases that would not have come to the surface otherwise.

The use of plant medicine for trauma and depression is evidence-based (so much research to support its efficacy) and even used for veterans. It's sad to me that it is not readily accessible for everyone and that there is still stigma around it.

Everyone's experiences and grief journeys are different, but I firmly believe plant medicine deserves a place on the menu of offerings to help people who are suffering.

Noah had asked to try psychedelics not long before he transitioned. I said no because it scared me. I didn't know much about it. But now, I wish I had investigated more. I wish I had given him the opportunity to do this deep inner work. I think now, he is showing me the way.

April 5

Ladybugs have been one way Noah comes to us. Today, a ladybug spent a solid twenty minutes going from arm to arm, keeping me company and putting a smile on my face.

Some days I feel his energy palpable in the space next to me, outside of my body. Some days I feel his playful energy inside of my body, intertwining with my own energy. Some days his energy comes through a visiting creature. Some days he visits in my dreams. Some days it's a flicker of the lights. Some days it comes through cloud formations or synchronicities or something somebody says that I know was meant for me.

Noah is so powerful. Our intertwined and never-ending love is overwhelming. My ability to connect with the energy of pure love is almost unimaginable. The perfectly orchestrated universe is awe inspiring.

Thank you. Thank you. Thank you.

I love you.

April 6

"Is that so?"

I've been listening to Ram Dass's talks this past week, and in one, he told a story about a spiritual teacher in a small town that everyone in the town loved and respected. At one point, the teenage neighbor got pregnant and told her parents it was this man's baby. The parents came and yelled at him, accusing him of sleeping with their daughter. He said, "Is that so?"

The whole town shunned him, and no one came to visit him anymore. He thought to himself, "Is that so?"

When the baby was born, they said it was his responsibility and left it with the man to care for. He said, "Is that so?" and took loving care of the baby.

A year later, the girl confessed that it was actually a poor young man's baby, and the parents came back to apologize and took the baby back. And he said, "Is that so?"

Not once did he become irate, defensive, angry, or worried. His ego was not there. The core of who he is—who we all are—was there. The presence of love, peace, and acceptance.

I was then observing myself and others this week with that lens. We get so riled up about so many things that we've declared as good or bad.

How could that person treat me that way? After all I've done, I deserve more. A massive resistance to the aging body not being able to do what it is used to. A turmoil inside of us at the state of the country. An ex-spouse making things difficult, a resistance to the reality of a terminal illness or death ... the list could go on ad infinitum.

As I observed, I thought about how much peace we could have if we accepted things as they are, without judgment of good or bad, or resistance to an outcome that is not what we wanted. What if we could say and truly feel in our hearts the detached acceptance of situations, and observe our situations as neutral, with an "is that so" approach? How amazing would that be?

I really like the state that this reflection puts me in. It helps me flow. It reminds me that everything is as it is. It's neither good nor bad. Our ego minds are just very effective at creating these dichotomies that promote suffering.

Is that so? I love you.

April 7

It's all real.

In my quest to understand what happens after your physical body dies, I've gone back and forth between Earth life being real and infinite spirit life being real. I had landed on infinite spirit life being real, and Earth life being some kind of weird matrix that we're in.

But now I know that it's all real. It all matters. It's all sacred. Our human bodies and lives, our struggles and our triumphs are all created from the same beauty and couldn't exist without each other.

That our infinite energy is real. That multiple realities can all be real and true at the same time.

That what is "real" is beyond our human brain's capacity to conceive. That we might just have to have faith and not know everything.

Faith. Surrender. Trust.

It all has deep meaning. Everything, everywhere, all at once.

I love you. I love me. I love us.

April 8

"When I don't know who I am, I serve you. When I know who I am, I am you." —Hanuman in the Ramayana

There are so many layers to awakening. I keep feeling like I have it, and then I realize I've just reached another step. And another step. There seems to always be more.

Unconsciousness.

Lifequake suffering.

Presence.

Awareness.

Contemplation.

Seeking.

Ritual.

Worship.

Presence.

Going within.

Shedding the feeling of needing confirmation outside of myself.

Realizing that I am, you are, and we are ... nothing and everything all at the same time.

Faith.

And back to presence.

An ever-deepening spiral of awakening while being human. Who knows what's next?

It's sort of a fun game, when you finally decide to really engage and play. Scary and fun at the same time—as is with everything, it can't be one without the other.

April 9

I've been told I'm an overthinker. I've thought a lot about that, and I'm not quite sure how I'm supposed to fix that. There are days I wish I could just chop my head off and live with my heart.

I've worried I don't do enough or I do too much or I'm not doing things right. It's hard to find the middle ground.

Everything seems to be a paradox lately. I clearly see that "trying" to be chill is not the way to go. "Thinking" about how I can stop thinking doesn't seem sane.

I internally know that feeling into the body more, taking life's challenges and opportunities one step at a time, and surrendering to the flow of energy is the way to go.

Now, (I think) it's just practicing doing that more each day. Surrender to the heart and flow somehow sounds easy, but it is most definitely the hardest challenge of my human life.

Month
10

April 10

Intense human feelings allow us to feel the full spectrum of emotion. My heart has shattered from heartbreak. It has exploded with love and gratitude. My body has melted into a puddle of despair. My stomach has formed into a ball of fear. My throat has constricted with anguish. My jaw has hardened with anger.

So much clinging and gripping. To both what my mind has deemed beautiful and horrible.

Is this all from the human ego? These intense emotions? If the human ego is stripped away, what does love actually look like?

Does it look like an even, calm, flowing state of acceptance and compassion? Not at all intense. Without attachment. Easy. Just there. Always present. Without reaction.

Why does this loss of intensity, when I think about how I have felt love, seem like a loss? It is a transformation of how I see love. How I have experienced love.

What would this new love look like in how I love and grieve Noah? What if I settled into this ever-present love without the grasp and strong hold of intensity?

How might this love transform my human relationships? With others and with my own human self?

This new experience and definition of love is blowing my mind. I'm humbly realizing that the truth of life has so much it keeps revealing to me. Infinite truths, infinite possibilities, infinite love.

It takes a leap of faith to fall into this abyss of infinite realities, trusting that it will catch me in this loving awareness and I don't have to hold onto all of the intensity to continue to exist, to continue to feel and be love.

I am. You are. We are. Love.

April 11

A wise guy in my life recently observed that every emotion in life stems from either love or fear.

It made me contemplate the difference between:

- Love and Fear.
- Pain and Bliss.
- Everything and Nothing.
- Reality and Creative Imagination.
- Surrender and dying.
- Infinity and an abyss.
- Suffering and Expansion.

Such a fine line ... and all are necessary to understand who and what we are.

Building on yesterday's thought—a clinging love, and tight grip love—is that not actually fear? When we lose the fear—fear of losing someone, fear of being hurt, fear of being alone—what is left?

I think it's just being. Being loving awareness. Being love.

This is not an easy task, to give up fear. But might just be one of the most important things we can contemplate while in our human form.

It takes a leap of faith.

I'm leaping.

April 12

The space in between.

We often feel consumed and immersed in our thoughts, our day-to-day activities, our problems, our suffering, and even in our pleasure. We become one with it all.

When we become one with something, we become attached to it. Becoming attached to things that are not permanent is suffering-making. We know that all things in material form, in this world of form, are impermanent.

We know that the space in between is always there. Just there, being. Calm. Present. Aware.

This is what meditation is supposed to do—show us the space between. Show us that we are not just this body on this Earth experiencing these highs and lows. This is also what plant medicine can show you.

This space of just "being" is what we are at our core. It's what allows for the creation of form. It is what allows everything else to come into creation. Without the space in between, there would be nothing.

When we think that our material world is everything, we become quite serious about it. When we can step back and see the space around it, knowing that in the space there is peace, we can see the absurdities of life and the craziness that we create ourselves due to this obsession with material form. It can become humorous to observe how we behave when we forget that we are more than our bodies, more than our actions, more than humans on this Earth.

It's all about perspective. Do I choose to be consumed by and immersed in material form, or do I choose to be the space in between, the peaceful observer? Marveling at the creation and transformation of form, watching it come and go in beautiful harmony. Still fully experiencing it all—but from the peaceful and non-attached space in between.

April 13

I am seeing how every day, every moment, every opportunity, and every challenge is my teacher. I have countless opportunities to practice living life from a soul's perspective. This is what we're here in human form for.

I don't want to waste a second! Instead of wishing I wasn't in human form, I want to maximize my time on Earth, learning from and experiencing it all.

I am practicing ...

Seeing myself and everyone else as more than their crazy, human, ego mind and human body. Seeing everyone as the spark of light that they are. Integrating the knowledge that opposites are needed to fully know anything and everything. The lightness and the darkness are all necessary.

I can continue to shed layers, and with each layer shed, I can hold more light than darkness.

Zooming out to observe it all from the space in between form and formless.

Seeing things without judgment, not good or bad. They just are. All is in divine order.

Practicing letting energy flow through me instead of gripping, clinging, and trying to force things to be as I want them.

Surrender and lean into every emotion. Surrender allows energy to move and not stay stuck.

Not taking everything so seriously. Seeing life as the playground that it is. Lightening up enough to play!

Nothing is permanent. Everything in form is transient. Allowing everything to come and go.

Noticing my human reactions—annoyance, impatience, hurt, passion—with self-compassion. Practice observing and letting it go.

Just being. Love.

I couldn't imagine this journey nine months ago. Noah's journey has been a greater teacher than I knew was possible.

Thank you. Thank you. Thank you.

April 14

Noah was so good at playing. Being silly. Not giving a fuck. Using his body to the fullest. He was one of the most genuine and free-flowing people I've known.

When he was younger, he would have dance parties with Grant and Hope. I loved watching these parties—free-flowing, with no inhibitions. He lost a bit of that uninhibited nature as he grew into a teenager and would only grace us with his funny dance moves occasionally. But he continued moving his energy through his body in other ways.

Since Noah's transition, I have found it very hard to even think about dancing or moving in a joyful way, letting joy and positive energy flow through my body. It feels scary and like a very tall order.

But I also feel the call, the pull, to be in full expression of my energy through my body. I feel the energy wiggling and trying to move all of the way through my core. How do I do that when I am still processing my grief? How am I supposed to feel all of the joy and love that I have inside of me? How do I let that rise to the top and move? How do I fully open my heart?

I don't know the answer to that just yet, but I feel the nudge internally. I'm starting with small things. Shaking my body. Gentle yoga. Butterfly pose. Swimming. Small hikes.

I think at some point it might be a decision to take a leap into free-flowing joy. I know it's right there in front of me. It's my choice to open my heart to it or not.

April 15

Our problems aren't the problem. Our perspectives are the problem.

Things can change so drastically with a shift in perspective. Death and the fear of it seem to control most of our actions and much of our suffering. This may sound insane to many, but one of the tools I have used to calm myself down when I start to get scared about not being able to control situations or protect those I love is to picture everyone already dead. To picture people, plants and animals during their entire life cycle—from birth to decay. This helps me to normalize what is, in fact, normal. I told my guide about this and they told me this is actually a form of Buddhist meditation—to visualize death and become comfortable with it.

What if our perspective on death shifted and we weren't terrified of it? How would that change how we live? How we cling? How we suffer? How would it alleviate our anxiety and need to control?

Would it allow us to be our full expression of love, of being loving awareness, in flow, in surrender, with ease and softness?

April 16

Trust. Surrender. Receive.
Jumping off of the cliff and having faith.
Practicing being brave like Noah.

April 17

You never know what the future holds. Anything can happen. The only thing we have is now. A now that we let flow into the next now, and the next, and the next. No gripping or clinging.

This past week, I noticed my struggle with and my desire to surrender. To loosen my grip. To be chill. I have gone deep with IFS to understand the parts of me that are terrified of losing control (the illusion of it, at least). And I kept saying, "I know I need to just have faith and jump off the cliff, but that seems insane. Who jumps off a cliff without knowing with certainty that they will be caught?"

I say these words, but I know in my gut that I will never know anything for certain. And if I want to stay in the flow of universal energy and live a peaceful and loving life, having faith, surrendering, opening myself up completely, then jumping off the cliff is necessary. This is the choice I need to make instead of choosing to live in fear.

I've also been contemplating the human body's role in mind, body, and spirit work. Yesterday, at the end of a zip-lining adventure we did, we were presented with the opportunity to bungee jump. I have always said this is never something I would do. It is terrifying. But I couldn't ignore the very clear opportunity staring me in the face after my week of saying I'm scared to jump. It couldn't have been clearer (thank you, Noah).

I knew I had to do it. I needed to show myself I could have faith, surrender, and jump. I felt the urge to use my body to express my surrender and let my fear go.

The Universe had clearly put this in my path. I repeated the words faith, surrender, receive to myself over and over and felt a sense of peace and calm wash over me. What did I have to fear when nothing can destroy me? When I trust in divine order? When I have faith that I am okay no matter what? When my brain gets out of the way and I'm stripped down to my core. When I don't take everything so fucking seriously?

I jumped and burst into tears and laughter at the bottom.
My body and my soul needed that.

April 18

"We can talk until the cows come home."

I've said over and over that no amount of talking could put a dent in my suffering.

After my latest plant medicine journey, I jokingly said to my guide that I couldn't believe he was walking around knowing what he knew from these journeys and hadn't told me.

He said that you can talk until the cows come home about your problems or what has happened to you in the past, but that will only give you insights into why you act a certain way. This is great and useful, but we can't stop there. Talking about your problems doesn't change the paradigm from which you operate in life in general.

When we have the bigger picture, it allows for acceptance, forgiveness, compassion, understanding, and ultimately more love and peace.

What you experience from a journey are the same things many spiritual leaders teach. Some people are able to internalize these truths without plant medicine, but for me I've been needing to speed up the process because of my trauma and grief ... and maybe because my scientist/researcher brain has needed to experience the intangible and unknowable instead of only reading or hearing about it.

I share this because I believe the mental health paradigm that our society is currently operating in places a focus on more surface-level processing that doesn't go deep enough to lay a foundation that can end suffering no matter what has happened to you or what will happen to you in the future. It's the base knowing that makes everything make sense, the things we label as good and the things we label as bad.

This foundation is one thing that can help with the mental health crisis our kids find themselves in. I wonder if this foundation is laid in terms of how we talk about life and death, good and bad, etc. If we grew up viewing these things from a higher perspective, would we need less therapy, less plant medicine, and less reliance on spiritual leaders? I wish I had known this foundation myself so I could have laid it earlier for my kids, but I'm committed to doing it from here on out.

April 19

Noah came to me in a dream last night as his younger self. I got to hug him, as usual. Feel his skin, his bones underneath, his warmth. And I sobbed. Because love and pain can feel the same.

I woke up realizing I have found the life hack of all life hacks. It is absolute surrender and trust. A big part of this is knowing that nothing exists except for right now. I am so grateful to have found it.

I had a hard time understanding how one surrenders and also manifests, or stands up for themselves, etc. They seem to contradict each other. Tolle talks about just noticing when you have a reaction to someone or something. That's the resistance or the needing. You can notice something out of alignment or that you wish to have in your life and speak up or pursue it without an egoic reaction. Of course we need to take care of and advocate for ourselves and our kids, but we can take action without intense emotion. And if a situation can't be changed, then we accept and surrender to it.

We have opportunities to practice this everyday. When we're late for work, we receive bad customer service, we decide we need something in our lives and long for it, we feel outraged at politics, we are ill, etc. When we notice the reaction, we can then become the loving awareness energy, observing it all while not becoming one with it.

Be loving awareness while taking calm and measured action or surrendering and trusting.

"God, grant me the serenity to accept the things I cannot change. The courage to change the things I can. And the wisdom to know the difference." —Reinhold Niebuhr, "The Serenity Prayer"

April 20

Be Chill. Noah and the Universe have sent me this message over and over. To me, it means the following:

- Find time and space for stillness. This is when we can know ourselves as more than our bodies and egos.
- Not try so hard. Just let things flow.
- Not to worry, control, or resist. Trust in a loving Universe.
- To accept life as it is and surrender.
- To not assign meaning to everything. Just let it be.
- To be present in the now and not project into the future or lament about the past.
- To be light-hearted and allow play, joy, and creativity to pass through me and out into the world.

I love you.

April 21

Noah and I had a good one-on-one talk laying on the trampoline of the boat watching the moon rise on this trip. We talked about all of the possibilities in life. I knew he was trying to find some motivation ... passion ... direction ... and I always told him he was never stuck. I emphasize this to Grant and Hope as well. Even with the traditional school structure, which doesn't work well for many kids, there is always another way. Even if it means making some sacrifices.

Noah was already thinking about what his adult life might look like. He knew the traditional college, desk job, family, etc. was not his path. We brainstormed lots of alternative options that might light his fire.

I've always told my kids they can create the lives they desire. And I will always support a decision that is made in pursuit of passion and excitement. I'm team Noah, Grant, and Hope. Always.

Passion and excitement are the feelings we get when we know we're on the right track. When we can shine our brightest light to share with the world. It's how we feel when we're in flow with our soul's purpose. While work is required, it feels easy and joyful. When we combine our way of "being" in the world with a "doing."

Shine your light.

April 22

I used to want to be anywhere but my house. Anywhere where I wasn't alone with my feelings and thoughts.

I have taken a few trips as of late, and I'm noticing a pattern. When my body and brain are tired, and I haven't created time to be still, connect with myself and feel my emotions, they end up coming out in hysteria in a restaurant, train, or airplane. My flashbacks increase and the intensity of my emotions increases exponentially.

I think I'm only doing "as well" as I have been because I am still so much of the time in my normal life. I'm present with my emotions. I feel in bits and pieces. Like letting little bits of steam out of the pot over time. I spend hours each day connecting with myself and with spirit. Noticing what is coming up for me each day. Feeling it. Moving through it. Writing. Journaling. Meditating. Sleeping/dreaming. Feeling my body through gentle movement. Slowly, slowly, slowly.

When I'm too busy to be still, it's not a positive "distraction." It's a numbing distraction that creates an environment for my grief to build until it explodes, and I'm one with it. I'm not in the awareness and observer role anymore. I've instead turned into a grief monster.

Full attention is full acceptance, is surrender.

I'm realizing that prioritizing stillness and managing my grief in bite-sized pieces seems to be best for an overloaded system. A system going through so much transformation.

Stillness. Feeling. Connecting. Zooming out. This is how I prioritize my time.

April 23

It was a cloudy day in New York. Not a chance of seeing the sunset. I could have assumed the sunset didn't even happen.

Then we rose above the clouds and a different perspective emerged. The sun was in fact setting, and it was beautiful.

Sometimes we don't see things that are just out of view. Or we see things from an angle that creates a totally different visual reality than someone viewing it from a different angle.

I'm constantly reminded that perspective is everything, and to not discount that anything is possible. That just because I can't see it with my eyes, or feel it with my hands, it's not real. Or because I see it one way, that that's the only way.

Anything is possible, if we're willing to allow it to be. There is magic everywhere.

What we focus on expands. What happens if we don't focus on any one thing, but soften, relax, and open to allow things we could have never even imagined with our current experience and paradigms to show up?

What if life and death isn't as scary as we make it out to be? And there is beauty everywhere, even where we currently see despair and sorrow?

What if everything is so much bigger and more beautiful than we could ever imagine?

Can you zoom out and open yourself up to the wonder of it all?

April 24

I've been using the words acceptance and surrender a lot. And I think for a while I thought that acceptance meant acceptance of the situation, which would eventually lead to me feeling no negative emotions.

But I'm seeing now that acceptance is the acceptance of everything—the past and the present. And all of the emotions that come with that.

The second I lean into my heartache instead of resisting, the softer it gets. And when I find softness, I can find peace.

I will always feel the full range of human emotions—no matter how "awakened" I become. The key is to surrender to, allow, and accept them all.

I had an epiphany about this the other day. Hope and I were in the middle and window seats on the way back from NYC. She had to pee, but the woman in the aisle was fast asleep with headphones in. Hope vacillated about trying to wake her up, thought about climbing over her, etc. And it occurred to me that this was a perfect metaphor for basically every situation in life. She could either do something about it (wake her up), or she could accept and surrender to the fact that her bladder was going to hurt until we landed in five hours. Anything in between is suffering.

Does acceptance of this fact mean that her bladder doesn't hurt? Nope. Does it mean that all of a sudden she doesn't have to pee? Nope. It just means that she chose to accept reality. In this case, she could have chosen to do something about it by waking her up, but sometimes in life, like when someone physically dies, there is nothing to be done. Acceptance and surrender are the only options. Does that mean I don't miss Noah, feel deep sorrow, ache, etc.? Nope. It means I allow myself to feel it all, instead of pushing it away in the hope that somehow it will be different.

It's the Chinese finger trap of emotion—pull and resist and you will create more tightness and stay stuck. Lean in to the hardness, soften, and you can find release. I love you.

April 25

Happiness vs. Peace

"I deserve to be happy."

I used to say this and believe it. Happiness was freedom, living where I wanted, doing the work I wanted, seeing my kids happy and healthy, having a near perfect romantic relationship, having enough money, traveling, etc. Now, I see happiness as a fleeting thing, and not at all the purpose of life. Happiness is fun to experience as a human, but it comes and goes as people, places, experiences, and things will inevitably come and go from our lives.

Happiness is only capable of being a "thing" because the opposite emotions also exist. How would we view happiness if we had never experienced sadness? Would it even exist?

Peace, on the other hand, is what you find when you accept all of the things that bring you happy or sad emotions that flow in and out of your life. Peace is found in acceptance and surrender. It's unflappable. It can't be taken away. If we've lost our peace, it is a mere perspective shift away from being found again. And when you have found it, you will realize it is the miracle of life. It is who we are on a soul level. Peaceful, loving awareness. Our human minds, consumed with being happy or not, have just become distracted by the illusion of needing to be "happy."

When peace is found, that is where you find joy. The joy of being. And watching. Seeing the beauty in all of it—the opposites interacting to create the excruciatingly beautiful and perfectly orchestrated mess of life. Acting as a vessel for life to flow through you in all its glory. There is no opposite to joy. It just is. It is not fleeting. It is our constant, if we allow it and let the pursuit of happiness fall away as the illusion that it is.

I love you.

April 26

Nine months have passed.

I don't default to waterproof mascara anymore.

I have smiled a big genuine smile.

Just this week I heard my excited energy through my voice for the first time. That used to be my signature thing.

I feel like I care about taking care of my body again.

I'm starting to think of other people more and make efforts to engage socially.

I'm thinking about cooking again.

I feel energy moving in me that will make me a better partner in my intimate relationship.

I'm not scared of the dark or being alone.

When my therapist asked how I was doing, for the first time I said, "I think, okay."

I have deeply sad moments and days. But I'm able to sit with them in a different way now.

I want to see how I can grow from life's challenges instead of die so I can have some relief.

Nine months without my boy with me in physical form.

Thank you, Noah. I love you, I love you, I love you.

April 27

I keep pondering what could have helped me help Noah. What can help me help Grant and Hope? What can I do to help the other kiddos I know who are struggling? Is it a book targeted at them? A podcast? A program through the schools? A campaign?

The more I work through these ideas, the more I think it's none of these things. Young adults aren't going to engage in these things, at least not the kids like Noah. And even if they do, it will be something in their life at a given time, not a solid foundation they can take with them forever. A "program" often becomes sterile, bureaucratic, susceptible to funding, and does not reach all kids. It's available for a limited amount of time and may provide a spark, but it will likely not keep the flame burning. I'm not saying programs can't be great, but I'm searching for something deeper.

I am confident that the best thing we can do is to help parents lead by example and be effective guides for their kids. I've said this before, but we are only a portal into the world for these unique souls in human bodies, starting their journey on Earth. We cannot control them, but we can be their loving guides. We can be a wise and open sounding board for them. We can show them what it means to live a life that is present and aware that we are more than our human bodies. That our realities are about perspective. That we can control our state of emotional well-being by giving up control and accepting the flow of life. That the most important thing is to find peace not "success." That they are whole and perfect already, and what society tells us about how our value is determined is suspect at best. That we value expressing creativity and joy. We can teach them the tools to connect with their inner selves by showing them how we do it.

To do this, we must heal ourselves. We must go deeper than coping and self-care strategies. We need to do the Soul Work.

This will change our kids. It will change the world. It all starts with you. Your well-being matters more than you realize.

I love you.

April 28

We can choose our perspective. One of the things I love about yoga is how we see our visual perspectives shift in each pose, depending on where our body is in space. It keeps you on your toes and reminds you that there is never only one right way.

I am having these huge shifts in perspective. Shifts that allow me to see the purpose in the light and the dark. To see the illusion of death for what it is. Shifts that allow me to feel connected to Noah. Shifts that allow me to give up the illusion of control and attachment. That allow me to feel amazing, powerful energy flow through me. Shifts that make my day-to-day life so much more full of joy and peace.

And then I find myself questioning if my perspective is real. Do people see me as a delusional grieving mom? It could very well not be real, maybe I'm just fooling myself so I don't suffer.

The truth is no one ever knows what's really real. We can only decide what perspective we want to live in. What our own reality is. It seems a bit silly to choose a perspective that creates suffering when we have an equal opportunity to choose a perspective that allows us to be at peace and feel joy.

Maybe I am just choosing a perspective that reduces suffering and increases peace to make myself feel better ... and why the fuck not?!

About the Author

Dr. Tiffany Ryan is a spiritual thought leader, licensed massage therapist, yoga instructor, and social worker with over fifteen years of experience in trauma-informed care. She holds a PhD and MSW in social work, with a research focus on child welfare and trauma. Her doctoral dissertation, "Comprehensive Child Welfare Policy Reform: An Analysis of Class Action Litigation's Longitudinal Impact on Child Outcomes," earned her the 2014 Society for Social Work and Research Doctoral Fellows Award.

After completing her PhD, and while working as a social work professor, Dr. Ryan pursued training in massage therapy and yoga in Costa Rica, aiming to deepen her understanding of the mind-body connection in healing. This journey led her to co-found Yomassage®, a modality that combines restorative yoga, mindfulness, and therapeutic touch in a trauma-informed manner. Most recently, after the loss of her oldest son, she has turned her focus toward the soul's role in living a meaningful life. As a result, she has created Yoga for Living™, a transformative, whole-person awakening path that supports individuals in navigating life's inherent suffering and challenges with gentle guidance to transform grief and suffering beyond acceptance and into a true understanding of your soul's mission.

Based in Portland, Oregon, Dr. Ryan spends her time with her earthside children and partner exploring the beautiful Pacific Northwest. She is involved in her community as a friend, author, educator, and speaker.